Writing Effective Letters, Memos, & E-mail

Third Edition

Arthur H. Bell, Ph.D.
Professor of Management Communication
Director, Communication Programs
Masagung Graduate School of Management
University of San Francisco
San Francisco, California

BARRON'S

All inquiries should be addressed to:
Barron's Educational Series, Inc.
250 Wireless Boulevard
Hauppauge, New York 11788
http://www.barronseduc.com

Library of Congress Catalog Card Number 2003062895

International Standard Book No. 0-7641-2453-6

Library of Congress Cataloging in Publication Data
Bell, Arthur H. (Arthur Henry), 1946–
    Writing effective letters, memos, & email /
    Arthur H. Bell.—3rd ed.
        p.   cm. — (A Business success guide)
    Includes bibliographical references and index.
    ISBN 0-7641-2453-6
        1. Commercial correspondence. 2. Memorandums.
    I. Title: Writing effective letters, memos, and email. II. Title. III. Series.

    HF5721.B483 2004
    651.7'4—dc22   2003062895

PRINTED IN CHINA
9 8 7 6 5 4 3 2 1

Contents

Preface

◆

This third edition, like the first two, aims to provide busy professionals with clear, easy-to-follow tips, strategies, and examples for successful business writing. Topic coverage has been expanded and refined in virtually all categories, especially the communication links made possible by fax and e-mail. Model documents show recommended writing principles at work.

The primary goal of this book remains unchanged: to help you write with ease, power, and skill.

Dozens of managers, executives, and business school professors have contributed their advice and insights to this new edition. Sincere thanks go to business leaders at Charles Schwab, Citibank, Cost Plus World Market, TRW, China Resources, Lockheed Martin, PricewaterhouseCoopers, Deutsche Telekom, American Stores, PaineWebber, Cisco Systems, Sun Microsystems, Genentech, and other major companies. In addition, the author expresses gratitude to academic friends and colleagues at Georgetown University, the University of Southern California, the University of California—Berkeley, Arizona State University, Portland State University, Old Dominion University, and the University of San Francisco for their interest and encouragement in this project.

Special thanks go to a superb editorial team headed by Linda Turner at Barron's Educational Series, Inc. These consummate professionals created a lively format for this book and resisted the author's temptation to go on and on. Certainly one of the attractions of the third edition is its brevity.

The author dedicates this work with love to his wife and dearest friend, Dayle M. Smith.

Arthur H. Bell, Ph.D.
Professor of Management Communication
Masagung Graduate School of Management
University of San Francisco
contact: bell@usfca.edu

Introduction

◆

What you write—and how you write—as a professional or businessperson stands as permanent testimony to your communication abilities, intelligence, and personality. Because you often write for your company as well as yourself, your words have lasting importance for what they authorize, explain, or promise. In short, you need to write well for professional success.

This third edition, including more than a dozen new techniques, examples, features, and shortcuts, puts you on the fast track for writing letters, memos, e-mails, and other business documents. Here you will learn to generate and organize your ideas quickly, choose document formats to achieve your purpose, and express your points clearly and persuasively.

Your path to becoming a superb business writer begins, in Chapter 1 (Your Style), with quick lessons on how to make your point in straightforward language. You can learn to write as naturally as you speak. In Chapter 2 ("Read Me" Layouts and Conventions), you will develop good instincts for choosing the shape and format for documents—that all-important look that communicates your professionalism. Chapter 3 (Recipes for Success) explains how logical, persuasive patterns of organization can be customized to fit your writing needs.

Remaining chapters lead you through the many types of written messages you undertake during your business day: good news, bad news, mixed news, informational messages, persuasive communication, and those challenging occasions when you must write under sensitive circumstances or at times of company crisis.

Although much has been added to this new edition, I have tried not to waste a single word. You are no doubt in a hurry to find practical solutions for writing problems and opportunities. Let's get started!

Chapter 1

Your Style:

The Natural Voice for Professional Writing

◆

Most of us in business swim in a sea of poor writing styles.

This chapter asks you to take a hard look at your writing style. Many business writers discover that the language they have been using for written messages isn't their own at all. They have been trying, perhaps for years, to sound like someone else. No wonder writing has often been a dreaded chore!

What is style? The short answer to that question is easy: style is *you* in writing. When you write naturally, you write with style.

The long answer to the question goes like this. Style is the window through which your reader sees what you have to say, your content. When that window is fogged over by dense, bureaucratic language, the reader may fail to see your point entirely. By contrast, a clear, easy style lets your reader look through your words, not at your words. Your intentions and meaning stand out.

STYLES WE LOVE TO HATE

Most of us in business swim in a sea of poor writing styles. The memos, letters, reports, and other communications we receive are often too long, too awkward, and too confusing for their own good.

Take, for example, the memos you receive from the *Bureaucrat*. His style never uses a short word where a long one will do:

> *"In accordance with prevailing company regulations in this regard, it is imperative that managerial facilitation pertaining to orientation of new employees be undertaken at all levels of authority."*

Say *what?* After reading (or attempting to read) this proclamation, what is a manager supposed to think or do? On the third or fourth reading, the intended meaning may emerge: "All managers must assist in new employee orientation."

Why didn't the Bureaucrat just say so? Probably because he thinks big words automatically create big thoughts and big importance for those who write them.

Not so. Busy professionals want letters and memos that seek to express, not impress. Few business people have the time or the patience to reread bureaucratic messages in search of the actual message.

A second too-common style is that of the *Windbag*. He latches onto a point like a Rottweiler and won't let go:

> *"There's a hygienic condition of concern not only to me but to all employees on the fifth floor. For the past several days, to my personal knowledge,*

> *and perhaps longer, according to people I've spo-*
> *ken with, the dispenser for paper hand towels*
> *next to the sinks in Room 368, the men's room,*
> *has remained empty of said towels and is at the*
> *present time still in need of refilling."*

The problem here is overkill. The Windbag cuts butter with an ax. If the message is simply, "The towel dispenser needs refilling," he should say so.

Finally, there's the style found in letters and memos from the *Hot-head*. These are the messages that, *a la* Clint Eastwood, "make your day": the angry, sarcastic, biting words that bring out the worst in every reader:

> *"Your presentation stunk. I told you NOT to use*
> *slides. Didn't you attend my training sessions on*
> *public speaking??? Obviously you weren't paying*
> *attention!"*

The style of the Hothead tempts a reader to respond in kind—as demonstrated in the "memo wars" so common in corporations. No style, in fact, is so costly to a company as the Hothead's style. It leads to precipitous actions, poor morale, unnecessary meetings and messages, and even transfers or resignations.

FINDING YOUR OWN STYLE
You know you're not a Bureaucrat, a Windbag, or a Hothead in your business messages. But you may not know who you *are* for writing purposes—what you should sound like, how your messages should appear on paper.

This misunderstanding leads directly to the nightmares of writer's block. We've all experienced the agony of false starts (or worse, no start at all) when an important memo or letter has to be written *now*. Or, after a promising beginning, we may hit the wall of writer's block halfway through the document. We read what we've written and moan, "This is all wrong. It isn't what I want to say."

At such moments, the culprit isn't lack of knowledge or a limited vocabulary. Writer's block occurs when we refuse to let ourselves *be* ourselves—be natural—in expressing our message.

Here's a case in point. Cynthia Maxwell recently was promoted to one of the vice president positions of a large Boston bank. "I had to write more," she says, "often in the form of messages directly to the bank president or the board of directors. I experienced an incredible case of verbal constipation. I wanted my writing to sound as prestigious as my new job title. But that kind of writing just wouldn't flow for me. I would begin, then fiddle with each word in the first sentence, then begin all over again."

Cynthia Maxwell rediscovered her own style when the chairman of the board told her, over lunch, that the board valued the K.I.S.S. principle above all others in communication: "Keep It Simple, Stupid!" All the bank president and the board wanted was Cynthia's clear thinking expressed as naturally and concisely as possible.

"Now," Cynthia Maxwell reports, "I imagine myself talking to my reader. That technique helps me get right to my point and say it clearly."

TEN FATAL ILLS IN BUSINESS WRITING

The "health" of your business writing can be threatened by the following common maladies:

1. *Anemic verbs* (is, are, was, were, seems to be)

   Not: It is the policy of this company to promote creative thinkers.

   Instead: This company promotes creative thinkers.

2. *Impotent verbs* (passive constructions)

   Not: The account was handled carelessly. (Note that the person who carelessly handled the account escapes visibility in this passive construction.)

   Instead: Jack Bevins handled the account carelessly.

3. *Atrophy of the position of emphasis*

   Not: There are two financial packages suited to our needs. (Note that the initial strong position is wasted on meaningless words.)

   Instead: Two financial packages suit our needs.

4. *Distended sentence length*

Not: While seven of our managers at the midlevel range object to the idea of moving our corporate offices, the majority of our senior staff is agreeable to the move and sees it as an opportunity to live in the Sun Belt.

Instead: Seven midlevel managers object to moving our corporate offices. Most of the senior staff, however, welcome the move as a chance to live in the Sun Belt.

5. *Hypertrophy of the noun*

Not: The unification of companies will prove beneficial to the establishment of financial arrangements more conducive to solvency and profitability. (Avoid multisyllabic nouns when possible.)

Instead: Merging our companies will help solve our money problems.

6. *Slow sentence pulse* Try mixing Subject-Verb-Object sentences with other types:

Frustrated, Jerry wrote a scorching memo. (*-ed* beginning before the subject)

The storeroom, long an eyesore on the fourth floor, is scheduled for remodeling . (Subject-Break-Verb)

His taxes are due, but his wallet was empty. (Subject-Verb, then Subject-Verb)

7. *Obese paragraphs* Try "easy in and easy out," using very short paragraphs at the beginning and end of business letters, memos, and e-mails.

8. *Noun clots*

Not: Please write a minorities opportunity evaluation report.

Instead: Please write a report evaluating opportunities for minorities.

9. *Spastic repetitions*

Not: We reviewed the benefits package. The benefits package provided for . . .

Instead: We reviewed the benefits package, which provided for . . .

10. *Contagious prepositions*

Not: We ran an advertisement in a trade journal in May for a manager of the sales division of our subsidiary in Wisconsin.

Instead: Use "Sales manager" and "Wisconsin subsidiary." (Combine prepositional phrases into adjective/noun combinations.)

◆

THE ELEMENTS OF A NATURALLY PROFESSIONAL STYLE

Simply describing a desirable writing style doesn't do us much good. Let's say, for example, that we agree that professional writing should be *concise*, *organized*, *natural*, and *appropriately friendly*. In fact, let's say that you memorized these qualities of style, repeated them to yourself whenever beginning a writing task, and named your children after them (Concisa, Organzus, and so on).

What has changed? Probably nothing. Knowing *about* style is like knowing about running. You have to "just do it," in the words of the Nike ad, to change your actual performance.

IN WRITING, WE ARE WHAT WE EAT

One way to turn buzzwords like *concise* and *organized* into reality in your writing is to see and follow good examples of these qualities. Unfortunately, most of us are surrounded by negative examples of business writing. Take a moment to glance over your inbox of messages from "upstairs" in your company—from your benefits office, from your legal counsel, from your training division, from your engineering staff.

Sadly, we swallow thousands of mischosen, misplaced words every business day. On such a diet, we may forget the pleasure of that rare business morsel: a crisp, clear sentence.

Worse, we may start to dish out the same verbal slop we receive. We receive a one-page memo that should have taken one paragraph, and respond to it in kind with our own page or two of gobbledygook. Not surprisingly, questions arise when the message is misunderstood. Meetings are necessary, as are more messages in writing and by phone. Office staff, along the way, requests overtime to deal with the extra keyboarding, photocopying, and scheduling.

The result? We come to think of corporate life as a stagnant swamp of inaction. We think of ourselves as mental mammoths caught in that swamp. And the company wonders why profits are slipping.

You can break the cycle of "garbage in/garbage out" by upscaling your verbal environment during the business day. Subscribe to (and read!) superb business writing, as found in *Fortune, Business Week, Forbes, Inc.,* and other popular business magazines. For models of specific business documents, build a small office library beginning with this book and also including some of the recommended titles in Appendix C.

By reading at least some good business writing each day, you can strengthen your ability to write naturally, clearly, and quickly—in short, your ability to write professionally.

USING YOUR COMMUNICATION TYPE TO ADVANTAGE

You have no doubt observed that different people take quite different approaches to initiating business communication. Some want to make "small talk" at first, with business talk reserved until a social comfort level has been achieved. Others set out a logical plan, with evidence, arguments, and a conclusion. Still others go straight to the bottom line, as if in a hurry to convey their core message.

These differences stem from individual communication types. Researchers beginning with the Swiss psychologist Carl Jung have defined and labeled these types in various ways. For our purposes, it is sufficient to focus on four main communication types. As you read the following descriptions, decide which type is closest to your communication habits and preferences.

The Thinker

The *Thinker* likes to think through problems to understand their causes and possible solutions. This communication type believes that communication is most persuasive when ideas are presented in a logical order, with appropriate supporting evidence. The Thinker often begins communication by trying to achieve agreement on a basic premise or set of ideas. Matters of opinion and feeling are of little interest to the Thinker, who seeks the "truth" irrespective of office politics and personalities. In attempting to prove his or her point, the Thinker will often use statistics, verified examples, and other sources of objective data.

The Feeler

The *Feeler* focuses on the emotional content of a situation—what people hope, fear, like, hate, accept, reject, and so forth. This communication type believes that communication is most persuasive when all involved feel relatively good about what is being said or decided. The Feeler often begins communication by trying to establish rapport in the form of small talk, engaging the listener's interests and feeling out the listener's mood. The objective truth of any situation matters less to the Feeler than its social impact and implications—how others respond and react. The Feeler often attempts to make his or her points by reference to personal emotions, anecdotes about how others feel, and broad appeals to "what will work for all of us" but is suspicious of so-called objective data, viewing it as a false front behind which others hide their real motives and feelings.

The Juggler

The *Juggler* always has one eye on the clock, schedules, deadlines, and budgets. This communication type takes pride in being able to take on several tasks at once. Often these tasks are not completed as thoroughly or carefully as others might do them, but the Juggler points to the emergency circumstances involved or the lack of any help to justify his or her shortcuts. The Juggler is usually the first to respond creatively and energetically to unexpected changes. The Juggler's solutions to problems are sometimes band-aids rather than true cures, due in large part to the Juggler's rush to judgment in finding answers. Some people rely on and even admire the Juggler for his or her ability to get so many tasks done in a short period of time. Others respond less positively to the Juggler, feeling that his or her accomplishments are half-baked and flawed.

The Planner

The *Planner* can relax only when daily events and tasks have been organized into a sensible pattern or plan. This communication type uses flow charts, diagrams, timelines, and other graphic aids in an attempt to capture and demonstrate "the big picture" to others. The Planner often initiates communication by a request that "we develop a workable plan" and may be unable to accomplish much work until such a plan is in place. At his or her best, the Planner aids the organization by increasing efficiency, eliminating redundancies, and enabling resource allocation. At his or her worst, particularly at times of organizational crisis or change, the Planner in his or her insistence on models, patterns, and plans can stand in the way of those trying to act quickly and creatively to counter threats to the organization, seize market opportunities, and resolve crises.

Which Are You?

Probably each of us carries a few qualities from each of these communication types. But in most cases, one type will predominate over others in our day-to-day communication and relations with others. (Tests are widely available to help you determine your type, including the Myers-Briggs Type Indicator.) But if you are aware of your usual approaches to problem solving and communication, you probably don't need a test to determine your dominant communication type. To double-check your findings, discuss the question of your communication type with a trusted friend who knows your habits well. He or she can be a valuable resource in helping you settle upon the type that fits your behavior best.

Your Communication Type

Having an accurate grasp of your communication type allows you to strategize well for communication with others. Here are two examples of such strategies, each for a different communication type.

When a Thinker Meets a Feeler In writing a memo to a Feeler or preparing for a conference or meeting with this person, the Thinker knows in advance that an absolute focus on logic and rationality, no matter how skillfully developed and presented, will fall flat—unless, of course, a bridge of sorts can be built to connect to the interests and preferences of the Feeler. Notice in this brief dialogue how the Thinker attempts to adapt to the communication style of the Feeler:

Thinker: John, I have three solid reasons for wanting to promote Susan to supervisor. But I know you're concerned about how her peers will feel. Shall we talk about that first?

Feeler: Great. If we can figure out a way to avoid jealousies and hurt feelings on the part of her peers, I have no problem with the promotion.

When a Juggler Meets a Planner Jugglers and Planners are traditionally at loggerheads with one another. The Juggler seems too shallow and frenetic for the Planner; the Planner seems too inflexible and uncreative for the Juggler. Notice in this brief dialogue how the Juggler adapts to the style of the Planner at the outset of the communication:

Juggler: Linda, I've got to catch a plane in half an hour, but I wanted to touch base with you about the marketing plan for the XYZ product. Instead of rushing right now, can I get some time on your schedule when I return so that we can talk out all the details in an orderly way?

Planner: That sounds great. I'll check my schedule and e-mail you with a few possible times and dates for our meeting.

In these dialogues, no one has permanently given up their own communication type in order to communicate with someone of a differing style. Instead, one person has made the effort to adapt to or build a bridge toward the communication preferences of the other person. These adaptations prevent the kinds of confrontations that impede communication—as, for example, when a Juggler rushes into the office of a Planner with a hit list of three decisions that must be made right away. Those kinds of encounters are sure recipes for misunderstandings and frustration for all concerned.

BUILDING STRONG COMMUNICATION TEAMS

Many communications developed in organizations, including reports, presentations, and proposals, are the combined work of a team rather than of an individual. Knowing the communication types of the individuals available for team membership can help a manager or supervisor ensure productivity rather than stalemate from the team.

Imagine, for example, a team made up exclusively of Planners. Surely the team members would have a firm set of guidelines, timelines, and schedules worked out. But they may not be so skilled in adjusting to sudden changes (the talents of a Juggler) or in "selling" their ideas to the rest of the workforce (the talents of the Feeler). Similarly, a team made up exclusively of Feelers would have good relations with one another and the rest of the workforce, but may not come up with logical ideas (as a Thinker would) or workable plans (as a Planner would).

Strong teams emerge from a combination of communication types. Each communication type brings a unique perspective to the task of the team—in effect, seeing the work at hand through a different window. When team members are aware of their own strengths as well as the complementary strengths of other team members, they come to appreciate the perspectives and agendas that others bring to the table. As a well-rounded team, the group is more likely to develop a work product that reflects a broad consensus in the organization rather than a narrow view. The group is also less likely to overlook important aspects or details of the subject at hand.

SUMMARY KEYS FOR YOUR STYLE

1. Using your natural voice in business writing will help you communicate sincerely with your readers and avoid writer's block.

2. The Ten Fatal Ills in Business Writing provide specific techniques you can use to write professionally.

3. Knowing your communication type allows you to make strategic adjustments in your writing for readers whose communication types differ from your own.

Chapter 2

"Read Me" Layouts and Conventions:

Eye Appeal for Persuasion, Including Fax and E-mail

◆

The medium is the message.

Marshall McLuhan

This chapter looks at the gift wrapping you've used to package the message you're presenting to your reader. Is that package attractive and easy to open for your reader? Or have you inadvertently spoiled your message by putting it in the wrong box?

Try this experiment with the next business letter or memo you receive. Glance at it just for a second or two, then put it aside to answer these two questions:

◆ Did the message appear to be important? What initial clues revealed the message as either hot stuff or junk mail?

◆ Did the message appear easy to read or tough sledding? Again, what clues led you to form your early estimate of its readability?

Your very first conclusions about a letter or memo have much to do with *a)* whether you read the message at all; *b)* how you look upon the message sender; and *c)* how you interpret and act upon the message itself.

Consider your probable response to a page filled by one gargantuan paragraph, printed singlespaced. No headings help you focus on highlights; no bullets or numbered lists help you make sense of items in series. You conclude, justifiably, that you don't *want* to read this message. If you must read it, you do so in a negative frame of mind that may influence your perception of, and response to, the message content.

Marshall McLuhan championed a principle important for every business writer: "The medium is the message." McLuhan points out that the medium of a letter or memo—its form on the page, its length, its printed appearance—is a vital part of the message being communicated.

Take, for example, the book you're now reading. Would it communicate as well to you if you were reading the same words in mimeographed or handwritten form? Publishers and authors know the importance of book design—everything from the book cover to the chosen fonts and line spacing—to make words credible and lively. In the same way, you can design your letters and memos for best effect.

CONTROLLING YOUR MESSAGE LAYOUTS

If you routinely give a draft of your letter or memo to a secretary for revision and rekeying, you may feel that the ultimate appearance of your message on the page is somewhat out of your control.

A secretary or other staff member may routinely decide what document format to use, how long paragraphs will be, and where white space will occur. More than one manager has been ruefully surprised to see, in the final printed version, how deadly dull a dictated message appears to be.

For successful letters and memos, you must take control of the *printed appearance* of your messages, not just their content. We're not suggesting that you must key in your own documents, although more and more managers find themselves doing just that. You must, however, let secretaries and other staff members know your wishes regarding layout, paragraph length, text placement, font size, headings, and related matters. Whenever possible, make these requirements known before rather than after the document has been word processed.

If you dictate, simply let your secretary know what letter or memo style you want (several styles are described in this chapter); where you want to end paragraphs; where you want a bulleted or numbered list set off by white space on either side; where you want inset margins; and where you want larger or smaller type sizes and different fonts. This added bit of work on your part will pay large dividends in creating effective business messages.

BUSINESS LETTER LAYOUTS

In the first years of the new century, the most common letter layouts (in order) remain the block style, modified block style, and simplified style. Companies and government organizations usually prefer one of these forms over others, or particular forms for specified types of communication. Sears, for example, typically uses block style for letter communication with customers and simplified style for correspondence with suppliers.

But wait a moment! Haven't business letters now gone out of style in most companies? Don't we use fax and e-mail for virtually all written correspondence?

Not at all. If you receive correspondence from an attorney, it will probably come in the form of a letter. If you receive notification of a scholarship award, a change in your benefits plan, a product recall, an upcoming city council meeting, or an overdue library book, it is likely that this information will come in the form of a letter. And, or course, junk mail letters remain extremely popular, at least for the sender of such letters. As the increased volume of stamp sales at the U.S. Post Office demonstrates, letters of all kinds are alive and well in the first decade of the twenty-first century.

What has gone out of fashion, unfortunately, is the competence in writing well-formed, persuasive business letters. Too many people attempt to apply e-mail writing habits to the composition of a business letter. This chapter, along with later chapters, aims to make sure that your business letters reflect well on you and on your company. Although you may write only one business letter for every 100 e-mail messages you send, that single letter may rise far above your e-mails in its importance to a crucial business matter, a sensitive personnel decision, or a delicate negotiation. Letters remain the highest (and most demanding) form of corporate correspondence.

Take the preferences and traditions of your organization into consideration when determining which layout to use for your letters. No one style is right or wrong; each has strengths and weaknesses, as explained below, that must be weighed in relation to your purpose and audience.

BLOCK STYLE

This style is used in approximately 80 percent of all business letters, perhaps because it is so easy to teach to office staff. As shown below, all letter elements are placed flush against the left margin. The letter body is placed so that it straddles the middle of the page. For letters longer than one page, the letter text on the final page begins after the top margin and is not centered vertically on the page.

Block style has the advantages of ease of preparation and a brisk, business-like appearance. Some writers feel that its lack of balance on the page (all elements, after all, are pushed to the left) may not be appropriate for more social or persuasive uses of the business letter. You may not want to use block style for readers more familiar with other styles. These readers include older persons, who grew up with indented forms of letter writing, and many international readers.

EXAMPLE OF BLOCK STYLE

(letterhead centered on page)

March 15, 20__

Ruth Foster, Manager
Conway Construction, Inc.
2983 Western Highway
Cincinnati, OH 60232

Dear Ms. Foster:

Last week you asked me to review letters sent from your company and to recommend a standard letter format for use by your employees.

More than a dozen variations of business letter format appeared in the 200 Conway letters I reviewed. When employees are free to choose or invent their own letter formats, the company suffers in three ways:

◆ Readers look upon nontraditional letter formats as errors.

◆ Readers infer a lack of coordination at Conway based on wide variations in letter style.

◆ Conway employees spend extra time converting letters from one format to another when letter texts must be revised.

For general correspondence at Conway, I recommend the block letter style, as described in the enclosed book, *Writing Effective Letters, Memos, & E-mail.* I believe you will find this style helpful in communicating a consistent company image through your correspondence.

Sincerely,

Robert D. Johnson

Robert D. Johnson
Communication Consultant

RDJ/coe

Enclosure: *Writing Effective Letters, Memos, & E-mail*

◆

MODIFIED BLOCK STYLE

This style, for your parents' generation, was the predominant form for business correspondence. As such, it may remain the expected form for many older business readers. These readers may, in fact, look upon more contemporary styles such as block style and simplified style as relatively cold and routine in nature.

The modified block style is somewhat more difficult to use than block style. The person keying in the letter must locate the horizontal center of the page for the date and signature block. All other letter elements are placed against the left margin. In one popular variation of the modified block style, paragraphs are indented five spaces.

For some readers, the modified block style looks more balanced on the page and therefore more gracious or social in appearance. The modified block style is commonly used for correspondence between executive levels of management and for persuasive letters such as sales and proposal correspondence.

EXAMPLE OF MODIFIED BLOCK STYLE

(letterhead centered)

March 15, 20__

Mr. Herbert Reed, Director
Southern States Charities, Inc.
3923 Lee St.
Savannah, GA 29832

Dear Mr. Reed:

Thank you for your letter of March 8 in which you inquire about appropriate letter formats for use in your solicitation letters.

Although the block style is used for most business communications, I recommend a less common form—modified block style—as particularly suited to your use. Unlike letter elements in block style, the various parts of a modified block letter are balanced on the page. This more traditional look may strike your mature readership as more professional and less stark.

The modified block style is explained in the enclosed book, *Writing Effective Letters, Memos, & E-mail.* Please contact me if I can be of further assistance.

Sincerely,

Robert D. Johnson

Robert D. Johnson
Communication Consultant

RDJ/coe
Enclosure: *Writing Effective Letters, Memos, & E-mail*

◆

SIMPLIFIED STYLE

This final style is used in no more than 10 percent of all business correspondence. As is apparent in the example, the simplified style streamlines the business letter to emphasize content over more personal or complimentary aspects of the letter.

In placement on the page, the simplified style abides by the same rules as block style. All letter elements are placed against the left margin. Notice, however, that the salutation and complimentary close found in block style are missing entirely in the simplified style.

Obviously the simplified style is not the style of choice for correspondence in which interpersonal warmth and formal politeness are high priorities. But in routine or mass-processed mailings, the simplified style saves the reader and the writer time by getting right to the main message without preliminary courtesies.

This is not to say that the simplified style is (or has a right to be) inevitably impersonal. As in the example following, the reader's name can be worked smoothly into the opening sentences of the letter, serving the purpose of a traditional salutation. Note in this regard that the simplified style lets the writer avoid the problem of deciding between "Mr." or "Ms." for gender-ambiguous names such as Pat and Chris.

EXAMPLE OF SIMPLIFIED STYLE

(letterhead centered)

March 15, 20__

Pat Connors, Accounts Supervisor
Acme Training Supplies, Inc.
22 Richfield Plaza
Dallas, TX 29832

REQUEST FOR RECEIPT OF PAYMENT

In my last order for seminar materials, Pat, I neglected to request your receipt for my check to Acme dated Feb. 1, 2004 (no. 2382). The check has already cleared, but I need your verification of payment for tax purposes.

I understand that Acme plans to represent a number of business film producers beginning in late 2004. As soon as you know which film titles you will be offering, I would appreciate receiving a price list for purchase or rental.

I've valued our business association over the years. Thanks for your prompt attention to the receipt request.

Robert D. Johnson

ROBERT D. JOHNSON,
COMMUNICATION CONSULTANT

◆

In the same way, an expression of well-wishing in the last sentence of the letter can take the place of the complimentary close.

Note: Ragged edge formatting (in which the right edge is not justified) simulates a previous generation of typed letters. Some business writers and readers feel that the ragged edge format shows spontaneity and relative informality, as might be expected in many memos and business letters. The issue has certainly not been decided by thorough research. Perhaps the best advice is to follow the custom of your company, or your reader's company, in deciding between fully justified or ragged edge formats.

OTHER LETTER ELEMENTS

No matter what letter format you choose, you will probably have occasion to use one or more of the following additional elements. More, however, is not better. Use only those elements that are necessary for your complete business message.

The Attention Line

At times, you may be writing a company without knowing the name of the person who will be reading the letter. In such cases, use an attention line to direct your letter to the intended reader:

Victory Toys, Inc.
892 Jones Road
Westwood, CA 89232

Attention: Customer Service

The Reference Line

Many government organizations and some corporations expect that reference will be made at the outset of a letter to previous correspondence identified by code number or date. The reference line is usually placed after the inside address or, if an attention line occupies that position, under the date:

John Frederick, Manager
Wilson Autonetics, Inc.
19 Federal Hwy.
Seattle, WA 89232

Reference: your letter, May 17, 20__

(or)

Reference: letter #89A42

The Subject Line

As an aid to orienting the reader to the central message of a letter, a subject line is often placed just before or after the salutation. This letter element lends a somewhat formal or official tone to the letter, and therefore is often omitted in more sociable or persuasive business correspondence.

Joan Trent, Vice President
Reynolds Industries
892 Henderson Dr.
Las Vegas, NV 29832

SUBJECT: 20__ OSHA Revisions

Dear Ms. Trent:

(or)

Joan Trent, Vice President
Reynolds Industries
892 Henderson Dr.
Las Vegas, NV 29832

Dear Ms. Trent:

SUBJECT: 20__ OSHA Revisions

The Salutation

One common problem in completing the salutation occurs when the gender of the addressee isn't known. Don't guess with regard to "Mr. or Ms." when addressing letters to people with gender-ambiguous names (Pat, Chris, Dale, and so forth). Make an effort to determine gender by calling the person's company operator or secretary. Failing that, address the person in the salutation by their full name or by their job title and last name:

Dear Pat Connors:

Dear Supervisor Connors:

"Ms." should be used in the salutation to address all women except those who had indicated a preference, in their correspondence to you or other contact, for "Mrs." or "Miss."

The etiquette of salutations and other forms of address for military personnel, religious leaders, government officials, academics, and a wide variety of dignitaries is treated in detail in *The Chicago Manual of Style* (see Appendix C).

The Complimentary Close

Choosing the appropriate word to precede your signature should be a matter of strategy, not habit. Many business writers use the standby "Sincerely" (a perfectly appropriate complimentary close) long after their business relationship with their reader has warmed to the point of deserving warmer words:

◆ Regards,

◆ Best regards,

◆ Best wishes,

◆ With best wishes,

◆ All best wishes,

◆ Cordially,

You must be the judge to determine when these words can appropriately take the place of "Sincerely." Certainly if you address your reader by his or her first name in the salutation you can maintain the same friendly tone by a warm complimentary close.

Your Signature

Sign your letter with your usual business signature, even though it may differ from your professional name as typed beneath your signature. As a general rule, if you have addressed your reader by his or her first name in the salutation, sign the letter with your first name.

Sincerely,

Thomas R. Smith

With best regards,

Thomas R. Smith

The Reference Initials

Following the signature block, the author of a letter indicates his or her initials in capital letters without periods, then separated by a slash the initials of the person keying in the letter in lowercase letters. Alternately, a word-processing code can be used instead of the reference initials. The code indicates where in the company's disk storage system the letter can be found.

Sincerely,

Robert D. Johnson
Communication Consultant

RDJ/coe

or, in place of reference initials or in addition:

WP30A32

The Enclosure Notation

When additional materials are included with the letter, they are named by title (preferably) or by type. This practice helps the person who "stuffs" the envelope make sure that all intended materials have been included. It also helps the recipient of the letter to ask for materials by name in case they were inadvertently left out of the mailing.

Enclosure: "Opportunities in Bond Trading"

or

Enclosure: 20__ company calendar

The cc: and bc: Notations

The cc: notation stands for "carbon copy," a duplication medium used less and less with the advent of photocopying. The initials continue to be used to preface names of people who have received copies of the letter.

cc: Bob Owens, Linda Valencia, Tom Morgan

The bc: notation stands for blind copy. It appears only on a copy of the letter, not the original. On the copy, it prefaces the names of people who have received a copy of the letter without the knowledge of the recipient of the original letter. Some personnel actions, for example, require that copies of reprimand letters be sent to upper levels of management without notification to the reprimanded employee.

bc: Tracy Wadsworth, Personnel Director

The P.S. (Postscript) Notation

P.S. notations are common in junk mail solicitations, where they are used to highlight special offers or last-minute motivators and calls for action. In other forms of business letters, the P.S. notation should be avoided if at all possible. It signals the inadvertent omission of information from the body of the letter—an omission that can almost always be repaired without a P.S. if the letter is prepared using word processing. For example:

P.S. I'll be away from my office June 7 through June 19. My assistant, Bob Robbins, will be happy to assist you during this period.

Folding the Letter

Junk mail can usually be recognized by an off-center, sloppy fold. When your business correspondence arrives in a similar condition, the reader's associations are hardly to your advantage.

Take care, therefore, to fold the letter carefully according to one of these traditional procedures:

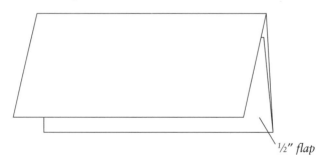

½" flap

Note in this fold that a flap of approximately ½ inch is left at the bottom of the folded letter to aid the reader in unfolding it.

The French fold is used particularly for window envelopes showing the name and address typed on the letter:

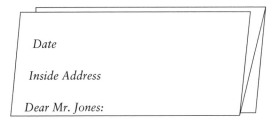

Date

Inside Address

Dear Mr. Jones:

Do not try to fold an 8½″ × 11″ letter to fit into a nonstandard or note-size envelope. Use a business-sized envelope or retype the letter on smaller stationery appropriate for the envelope size.

ENVELOPE CONVENTIONS

A standard-size business envelope is addressed as follows:

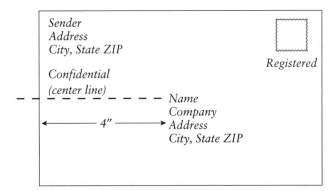

Sender
Address
City, State ZIP

Registered

Confidential
(center line)

Name
Company
4″ Address
City, State ZIP

Note that no information is placed lower on the envelope than the ZIP code line for the sake of automatic sorting machines at the post office. Any instructions from the sender such as "Confidential" or "Time-dated Materials" are placed beneath the sender's name and address. Any instructions for the post office such as "Registered" or "Do Not Bend" are placed under the postage, but not so close to the postage that these messages may be obscured by stamps or cancellation.

MEMO FORMAT

Unlike business letters, memos have remained relatively fixed in format over the past decades. Although the order of these elements varies somewhat from company to company, all memos begin with a block specifying (at minimum) the date, the intended reader, the memo writer, and the subject.

In the following sample memo, note that the body text is not centered top to bottom on the page. Many memo writers add their handwritten initials beside their name or at the bottom of the memo.

SAMPLE MEMO

Date: January 6, 20__

To: Linda Evans
   Vice President

From: Paul Ortega
   Sales Director

Subject: Arrangements for visiting Japanese managers

I've attached a suggested agenda for the twelve Japanese managers who will be visiting our headquarters on Jan. 18.

Their translator, Uko Katama, will accompany them on the plant tour. He will also be available, if you wish, to translate your welcoming speech to the group. It will be helpful for Uko to have a copy of your speech a few days before the visit.

All other arrangements are in order, I believe, for a productive day with these managers. Let's meet briefly on January 17 to handle any last details.

◆

MAKING THE MOST OF FAX AND E-MAIL CORRESPONDENCE

The increased speed with which we can now send and receive messages electronically has tempted some business writers to lower standards of quality, both in the content and format of messages. We have probably all received unreadable faxes—ones that have been retransmitted too often, or set in a tiny, hard-to-read font. And we have no doubt all suffered through interminable e-mail messages lacking paragraph divisions, headings, bullets, and even capital letters and basic punctuation.

If you intend your messages to be read, fax and e-mail transmissions must be given the same care as traditional correspondence. Employees at many large companies already find themselves swamped in electronic messages. Only the most readable survive as communications. At Sun Microsystems, for example, managers receive on average more than 100 e-mail messages per day. Messages that abuse the reader's time and patience—rambling, poorly formatted, and overly long messages—don't deserve and don't receive the same attention as clear, succinct messages.

Follow these common sense suggestions for preparing e-mail messages that succeed for you and your reader:

◆ Make every effort to keep your message to no more than one screen-full. When a message must run longer, consider sending a brief cover message and using the "Attachment" function for the longer document.

◆ Copy only those readers with a need to know. One study estimates that more than 70 percent of e-mail received by employees in major corporations is the result of misrouting or needless copying.

◆ Headline your e-mail message with a clear subject line so that the reader can get to the heart of your communication right away.

◆ Use paragraph divisions, bullets, indentation, headings, and any other format devices that make your message easy to read and remember.

◆ Make clear (usually at the end of the message) what you want your reader to do with your communication. Is your message for informational purposes only? Do you want a reply? Do you want action of some kind? Say so!

◆ Remember that your electronic messages create your image—professional or otherwise—for the reader. Manage your image as a communicator by managing how your e-mail messages look and read.

Facing Up to E-mail Realities

When we write an e-mail, we have a natural tendency to project onto others our own e-mail habits or the e-mail culture of our company. For example, if we tend to check our e-mail every hour or two (or respond as pop-up e-mail notifications arrive on our screen), we may expect the same e-mail diligence from our message receiver. In fact, we may make the mistake of counting on having our message read and responded to within an hour or two—simply because that's how fast we usually process our own e-mail.

In truth, many managers (and entire companies) are notoriously slow or unpredictable in handling their e-mail. One manager may let e-mails accumulate for a day or two before scanning them to pick out the most important for replies. Another manager may have installed a "bulk" filter that sends unsolicited messages (perhaps including ours!) unread to a low-priority storage file. Yet another manager may have delegated the initial sorting and review of e-mail to an administrative assistant, with only a few messages selected out for the manager's personal attention.

Given these many communication barriers, you must plan your strategy for getting your e-mail message through to its intended reader. Consider the following Do's and Don'ts:

◆ Do create subject lines that motivate the reader's attention.

◆ Don't scream "URGENT URGENT URGENT" in subject lines unless circumstances truly require that kind of alarm. Writers who overuse such language quickly find their messages ignored and even ridiculed.

◆ Do make a phone call to alert your intended message recipient that a particularly important e-mail has been sent.

◆ Don't duplicate your messaging unnecessarily (for example, by sending a fax, e-mail, and voicemail all containing the same message).

◆ Do use the cc: and bc: functions to send your e-mail to those with a need to know.

◆ Don't attempt to motivate a quick response from your reader by misusing the cc: and bc: functions as manipulation ("Look, I've let your boss know that I've sent a message to you. You had better respond right away!").

Principles into Practice

You may be unaware of your own e-mail habits from day to day. Take a moment to jot down answers to the following questions. Complete both the "What I do now" and "What I want to do" portions for each question.

1. On a typical business day, how often do you check your e-mail?

   What I do now:

   What I want to do:

2. When you check your e-mail, how do you decide which messages to respond to right away, which to delay, and which to ignore altogether?

    What I do now:

    What I want to do:

3. Do your habits for checking e-mail vary widely from day to day, based on your other commitments, schedule, and work flow?

    What I do now:

    What I want to do:

4. Are you able to check e-mail (perhaps by forwarding it) after work hours?

    What I do now:

    What I want to do:

5. What are the expectations of your company regarding the checking of e-mail by employees? How do you measure up to those expectations?

    What I do now:

    What I want to do:

Tips for Fax Messages

In addition to these points, observe a few extra guidelines when sending faxes:

◆ Choose fonts, letterheads, and colors that will fax clearly. As a general rule, no font smaller than 10-point should be used for faxed documents. Brown, red, and blue inks used in letterheads may not fax well.

◆ Remember that fax transmissions may pass through several hands—from mail room to office delivery to secretary, and so on—before reaching their intended readers. Be aware of who will see your fax before sending sensitive or confidential messages.

◆ Use a cover sheet containing the following information: the message sender's name, company, address, telephone number, and perhaps the fax number and e-mail address as well. Also provide a telephone number to call in case of trouble in the fax transmission. Indicate how many pages make up the fax transmission, including the cover sheet. Some companies also show the purpose of the message: For Your Information, Action Requested, Urgent Notice, and so forth.

◆ Be careful not to retransmit a fax message that already appears fuzzy on the page. Using standard fax machines, each successive transmission can blur the print by 25 percent or more.

These guidelines are must-do protocols, not nice-to-do matters of communication etiquette. Important business details and, indeed, major negotiations and deals may depend on clear, effective electronic messaging.

SUMMARY KEYS FOR "READ ME" LAYOUTS AND CONVENTIONS

1. Readers expect the use of conventional formats in letters, memos, and e-mails—and count it against your professionalism if you depart significantly from these formats.

2. Block style remains the most common format for business letters.

3. The blizzard of words surrounding virtually all business people requires that e-mail messages be concise, directed only to their intended readers, and formatted (in terms of subject line, use of bullets, and so forth) for easy reading.

Chapter 3

Recipes for Success:

Quick Plans to Clarify Your Writing

◆

Create a pattern that helps you say all you want to.

This chapter introduces shortcuts that help you spend less time writing while expressing yourself with more clarity and impact. The term *recipes* in the chapter title does not mean that you must follow a rigid formula when composing a business message. You are always free to depart from these guidelines as necessary to express what you want to say. But having general guidelines in mind can save you a great deal of time and effort as you plan your message.

Consider various forms of creation. To build a house, a carpenter follows blueprints. For a cake, a baker follows a recipe. Even nature follows the DNA code. Only the writer frequently insists on "winging it" without a plan when constructing the texts of letters and memos.

You've seen the result too often in your in-basket: disorganized, rambling messages that you must read two or three times to untangle.

And you're not the only one to pay the price for poor planning. The letter or memo writer probably struggled to produce the mess you hold in your hand. It's hard, after all, for a writer who hasn't planned what to do with his or her words to write well.

This chapter suggests five planning aids to benefit both the reader and the writer. These short recipes tell, paragraph by paragraph, how to develop a concise, logical message-text for letters or memos. Like all recipes, these can be varied to suit your individual needs.

HOW TO USE A MESSAGE-TEXT RECIPE

Before considering any recipe to guide your writing, review (out loud, if possible) what it is that you want to communicate. Then, with a firm grasp on your intended message, look over the following recipes. At least one should leap out at you as an ideal step-by-step agenda for writing your message-text.

Or you may find two or more recipes that can be combined to produce an order of ideas that suits your content. Your goal should be to find or create a pattern that helps you say all you want to, no more, no less.

PATTERN ONE—MESSAGES BASED ON TIME

In this pattern, the first paragraph should discuss what has occurred in the past. The second paragraph deals with the present. A final paragraph looks toward the future. In the following example, notice that an initial overview sentence has been added to let the reader know that time will be used to organize the message-text.

Uses: problem descriptions, brief histories, informational summaries with recommendations or forecasts.

Dear Mr. Forest:

As you requested, I've investigated the vandalism problem at Plant #6 for the period 2002 through the present. This letter summarizes my findings, with recommendations. A more detailed report will be forwarded to you early next week.

From the opening of the plant in 2002 through June of 20__, no incidents of vandalism were reported. That summer, however, the company purchased six vacant lots adjoining the plant for employee parking. These lots, it was later discovered, had been used for many years as a baseball and football field for neighborhood youth. From the summer of 20__ through last month, a total of 48 incidents of vandalism have occurred. These range from broken windows in employee automobiles to graffiti on plant walls.

At present, the company's executive council is involved in biweekly meetings with neighborhood representatives to resolve the ongoing vandalism problem. A total of seven private security guards now assist city police in surveillance and protection of company property.

Looking toward the future, we can predict further outbreaks of vandalism so long as the playground/parking lot issue continues to rankle the neighborhood. I recommend, therefore, that the company assist neighborhood representatives in developing a recreation area for its children. The expense of this worthwhile endeavor will prove to be far less than the costs of an ongoing struggle with the neighborhood.

◆

PATTERN TWO—MESSAGES BASED ON SPACE

In this pattern, the first paragraph deals with something at a great distance. The second paragraph focuses on something closer. The final paragraph discusses or describes something right at hand. In the following example, an initial sentence orients the reader to this far-to-near pattern of description.

Uses: informational descriptions, orientations, market analyses.

Dear Ms. Morgan:

We're happy that you will be joining us as a field sales associate. I'm writing to acquaint you in general terms with your regional, community, and business park sales territories.

Your sales boundaries extend from Chula Vista on the California/ Mexico border to Oceanside, and east as far as El Centro, California. We expect that major clients within this region will be visited at least once every two months as well as on an as-requested basis.

Your home base area is San Diego, where you will probably do 60 to 70 percent of your total volume. In organizing your time, please plan to spend at least two-thirds of your working hours within the city limits of San Diego.

The focal point of your efforts, of course, will be in the Santa Inez Business Park where your office is located. Over 400 potential clients are located within the park, and we know that you will pursue their business aggressively.

Ted Vickers, our western sales vice president, will meet with you next Wednesday to discuss company goals and sales strategies for your area.

PATTERN THREE—MESSAGES BASED ON CHANGING PERSPECTIVES

In this pattern, the first paragraph discusses how you once thought or felt about a subject. The second paragraph describes some crucial event or insight that changed your perspective on the subject. The third paragraph assesses how you now view the subject.

Uses: explanations, analyses, evaluations, personal disclosures, adjustments.

Dear Mr. Denton:

When I first read your letter of May 1 regarding a morning traffic problem in front of your home, I admit I felt skeptical. I couldn't imagine how the departure of our company trucks from the Seventh Street lot could block your driveway on Ninth Street, as you describe, for more than an hour each morning.

Two days after receiving your letter, however, I drove to work past your property. There, exactly as you said, were at least ten company trucks lined up at the Ninth Street/Western Ave. intersection.

The cause, we have since discovered, is a mobile diner located just past that intersection. Drivers were lining up on Ninth Street to buy coffee and doughnuts at the diner before beginning their daily routes. We've talked to the owner of the diner about the traffic problem, and I'm happy to report that he has relocated his operation to Seventh Street, where the line of trucks won't cause a problem.

Thank you for bringing this matter to our attention. We apologize for the inconvenience you've experienced and trust that the problem is now solved.

PATTERN FOUR—MESSAGES BASED ON CAUSALITY
In this pattern, the first paragraph discusses surface symptoms. The second paragraph describes immediate causes of those symptoms. The final paragraph deals with deeper causes.

Uses: personnel evaluations, problem analyses, sales and marketing assessments, trouble reports.

Dear Ms. Wenden:

After six successful quarters of sales in the Seattle area, we were both confused by last quarter's results: general sales down 16 percent, on average, across our nine area stores.

As we discussed by phone, some of this downturn can be attributed to layoffs at Boeing, the area's largest employer. During the quarter, Boeing gave layoff notices to approximately 5 percent of its workforce.

But it's dangerous, I believe, to assume that our sales slump is due simply to such layoffs. During the quarter, two powerful competitors—SaveMarts and Bargain Boys—opened a total of eight stores within the greater Seattle area. The grand openings of these stores were accompanied by their heavy advertising of sales items.

I recommend a thorough assessment of the impact of such competition upon our sales.

◆

PATTERN FIVE—MESSAGES BASED ON PROPORTION

In this pattern, the first paragraph tells what most people think or feel. The second paragraph focuses on the opinions of a smaller group. The final paragraph discusses the perspective of an even smaller minority or your own point of view.

Uses: meeting and discussion summaries, market descriptions and analyses, personnel and attitudinal evaluations.

Dear Mr. Evans:

I have polled company employees on the issue of flexible work scheduling. A total of 308 of the company's 445 employees responded to the survey form included with last month's paychecks.

Most employees (74 percent) favor flextime based around a core of required hours from 10 a.m. to 3 p.m. Under this plan, an employee could arrange his or her 40-hour week as desired, so long as the core block of required hours is included each workday.

A smaller group (20 percent) wants complete flextime without the core hours requirement. Many members of this group favor optional Saturday and Sunday working hours for job categories (such as programmers and systems analysts) not usually involved in interdepartmental meetings.

The remainder of those polled (6 percent) were opposed to flextime entirely. These employees (primarily managers) argue that their work will be made more difficult if employees are allowed to choose their own work schedules.

Based on the result of this thorough poll of employee preferences, I recommend that the company undertake a pilot test of the "core hours" approach to flexible work scheduling.

PRINCIPLES INTO PRACTICE

One way to persuade yourself of the importance of message patterns or recipes is to observe documents that lack such a plan. Take a moment to find a recent letter, memo, or e-mail (your own or someone else's) that seems to ramble for lack of a thought structure or pattern. Decide which of the five recipes discussed in this chapter (or another recipe of your creation) would help the document make its points more clearly and persuasively.

OVERCOMING RESISTANCE TO RECIPES

No writer likes to be told what to do, even by a helpful recipe. Use these patterns, therefore, to stimulate possibilities for developing your ideas, not as a straitjacket for your imagination. With practice, you will soon find yourself using patterns of thought almost unconsciously. At the same time, you'll find yourself writing much more quickly than ever before.

SUMMARY KEYS FOR RECIPES FOR SUCCESS

1. Using patterns for the development of documents helps the writer organize his or her material according to standard stages of argument. These patterns can be altered as necessary to fit the writer's purpose and audience.

2. A pattern helps the writer work quickly and avoid writer's block. The writer's points and supporting evidence can easily be categorized into the various parts of the pattern.

3. Basic patterns of argument explained in the chapter are patterns based on time, space, perspectives, causality, and proportion.

Chapter 4

Here's the Good News:

Letters, Memos, and E-mail That Say "Yes"

◆

What better time to nurture a good business relationship through well-chosen words of goodwill!

This chapter shows you how to write the most pleasant of business messages: those that say "yes" to your reader in one way or another. Through these messages you have the opportunity not only to earn the appreciation of your reader but also to express the kind of goodwill that builds relationships for future business.

At least half of all letters and memos written in business carry good news to the reader: yes, we have the products and services you need; yes, we can fill your order; yes, we can extend credit; yes, we can answer your inquiry; yes, we accept your invitation; yes, we will make an adjustment based on your claim.

The key to successful good news communications lies in using them to build goodwill. Readers are pleased, after all, to receive your "yes" message. What better time to nurture a good business relationship through well-chosen words of goodwill!

THE GOOD NEWS SALES LETTER
Your appropriate enthusiasm for your products or services can be contagious for the reader. There's a fine line, of course, between upbeat enthusiasm and "step-right-up" carnival behavior. Demonstrate the energetic, optimistic spirit of a winner in your sales letters to motivate your reader to say "yes" to your sales appeal.

As you consider the following letters, you may have second thoughts about whether you would put such information in a letter at all. Couldn't fax and e-mail be used to communicate more directly and inexpensively with your audience? Yes and no. Certainly e-mail and fax offer time and cost advantages over traditional letters. However, as legislation blocks unwanted fax transmissions and "spam" e-mail contacts and as software programs make it possible to screen out e-mail from unknown senders, getting your message into the hands and minds of your intended recipients (in short, communicating) may not always be easy by fax and e-mail. Don't underestimate the power of a well-written, crisply formatted business letter to convey your message and your company's image in an optimally persuasive way.

Notice in the following before and after examples how the good news tone increases the power and potential of the sales letter.

VERSION ONE: A LACKLUSTER SALES LETTER WITHOUT THE GOOD NEWS TONE

Dear Mr. Frank:

Since 1992, Union Tire Company has served the tire needs of this community.

During the entire month of May we are offering fleet managers a 15 percent discount on all tires and mounting/balancing charges.

To schedule appointments for your vehicles, please call Jeff Edwards, Service Manager, at 555-3892. Thank you.

Sincerely,

Tony Agnotti

Tony Agnotti
Sales Representative

VERSION TWO: A LIVELY SALES LETTER EMPLOYING THE GOOD NEWS TONE

Dear Mr. Frank:

At our lunch together last month, you asked me to let you know right away about any special promotions that could save you hundreds of dollars on tire replacements for your fleet.

I'm happy to send you this advance notice of Union Tire's May sale for fleet managers. We're offering a full 15 percent off all tires, including mounting and balancing charges.

I'll call you tomorrow to answer any questions you have about these discounted prices. With the green light from you, I will be glad to help you schedule your vehicles for installation of great tires at great prices.

With best regards,

Tony Agnotti
Sales Representative

◆

The point in these comparison letters is to remember the good news dimension of every sales letter. The product or service you are offering should be presented as a welcome answer to the client's need. As the salesperson, you can feel good about serving those needs—and your good feelings about yourself, your client, and your products or services should shine through in the tone of your sales letter.

GUIDELINES FOR EVALUATING YOUR AUDIENCE
Planning a document or speech requires your clear vision of what your audience needs and wants from you.

1. Evaluate the experience of your audience. Do your readers or listeners know background information necessary to understand your words? If not, what additional information should you provide?

2. Evaluate the intellectual level of your audience. Have you chosen words, examples, and arguments they will grasp?

3. Evaluate the time commitments and attention spans of your audience members. How much can they be expected to read or listen to?

4. Evaluate the predominant attitudes and beliefs of your audience. Will your point of view agree or disagree with their views? Which of their values, tastes, or beliefs can you use to support your argument?

◆

GOOD NEWS AND GOODWILL IN ROUTINE RESPONSES

In saying "yes" to a customer order or request, you have an ideal opportunity to build the kind of goodwill that promotes future business. Notice in the following letter to a new customer that the good news (the "yes" message) is followed by a bit of appropriate salesmanship for the company.

━━━━━━━━━━━━━◆━━━━━━━━━━━━━

Dear Mr. Cort:

Welcome to the Trevex wholesale outlet for more than 1,000 floral retailers. Your order, No. 2983, has been filled and will be delivered at your store on March 23 by 12 noon.

We will do whatever we can to deserve your continued business. Please call our customer hotline, (800) 555-9823, with any questions or concerns you have about billings, shipments, or special promotions.

To say thanks for your first order, I've enclosed a 10 percent discount certificate toward your next purchase totaling $800 or more. I've also sent along our summer catalog, with five "best buys" specials highlighted for your interest.

Best regards,

Lisa Browne

Lisa Browne
Sales Director

◆

In the following response to an inquiry, the writer turns a win for the reader (who receives the answer to a question) into a simultaneous win for the company by promoting goodwill.

Dear Ms. Underwood:

We were pleased to receive your inquiry (Jan. 2, 20__) regarding the propulsion specifications of the Z70 rocket engine manufactured by this company. Although some aspects of the engine design must remain classified, I have enclosed an engineering fact sheet providing the thrust data you seek for your thesis.

You may also be interested in viewing "Toward the Stars," a PBS production cosponsored by Space Design, Inc. This program, scheduled to air on Feb. 5, reviews the history of rocket technology and discusses many of the issues you mention in your letter. If you can't see it in your area, please contact me and I'll loan you a videotape of the program.

Thank you for your interest in our work and products at Space Design, Inc., and best wishes for success in your graduate studies.

Sincerely,

THOMAS B. WATSON

Thomas B. Watson
Public and Corporate Relations

The extra effort toward goodwill in the second and third paragraphs of this letter pays dividends for the company in several ways: one more member of the public is positively impressed by the company, a graduate student may well be attracted to apply to the company in the future for work, and the company's public service efforts via public television receive a bit of advertising.

In this credit communication, the good news of approval sets the stage for some direct marketing of specific products.

◆

Dear Mr. Richmond:

Lindbay Furniture Manufacturing is pleased to approve your revolving credit account #29832 in the amount you requested, $10,000. No interest will be charged on balances paid within 30 days of purchase. A sliding interest amount, as described in the enclosed credit disclosure, will be charged on balances exceeding 30 days.

With summer just a few months away, I'd like you to know about Lindbay's upcoming sale on its popular line of patio furniture March 10–15. Orders received for patio items during this period will receive a 10 percent discount. The enclosed catalog provides details on the patio line and convenient order forms.

We look forward to hearing from you and, again, our sincere welcome as a new Lindbay client.

Cordially,

Roberta Johnston

Roberta Johnston
Customer Representative

◆

SUMMARY KEYS TO DELIVERING GOOD NEWS MESSAGES

1. Show the kind of enthusiasm for your product or service that you want your reader to feel.

2. Present your sales message as a good news solution to the reader's needs or problems.

3. Build goodwill for your company by including well-wishing, expressions of appreciation, and other courtesies in even the most routine communications.

Chapter 5

Here's the Bad News:

Letters, Memos, and E-mail That Say "No"

◆

Saying "no" takes character.

This chapter reviews strategies and techniques for making the best out of less than ideal circumstances: those many times in business life when you must say "no" with conviction but without anger. In the previous chapter, we observed that saying "yes" in business messages can build good relationships. Saying "no," as discussed in this chapter, does not have to be destructive to work relationships—and can, if handled well, set the stage for better relationships in the long term.

You'll say "no" in business messages at least as often as you say "yes." Boss, can I have a raise? No, not this quarter. Can your company donate a pickup truck to the Boys Club? No, I'm sorry that we can't. Mr. Manager, I demand compensation for my mental anguish when your product failed. No, we aren't able to grant your claim.

Saying "no" takes character. You're risking angry reactions from those you refuse. They may dislike you—and tell you so to your face. They may talk about you behind your back, or send complaints to your superiors. They may take their business elsewhere.

For these reasons, some managers and other professionals have real trouble communicating bad news. They avoid such confrontations or delegate them to others: "Uh, Ms. Jones, would you take Mitchell aside and explain to him why I can't give him an extra week of vacation. You two seem to be friends." Or they try to disguise every bad news message as neutral or good news: "Mitchell, I'm going to get your input from now on when I draw up the vacation schedule."

The hard truth about bad news is that people will be disappointed. People may get angry. People may blame you. "Heavy lies the head," says Shakespeare, "that wears the crown." Part of the burden of leadership at any level is the necessity of occasionally communicating bad news.

But people prefer honest bad news to dishonest soft-soaping or manipulation. In asking for a price break, for example, a customer would rather receive a courteous turndown than an interminable series of lame excuses: "Well, if it were up to me, I would say yes, but I have to check with Mr. Allen, and he's out of town for several days. In fact, I'm not sure when he will be returning . . . "

This kind of stalling and waffling is business cowardice, not kindness. Customers and employees understand the fact that you have standards and limitations you must live by. They respect you when you're forthright about what you can and can't do. They resent being conned.

CONVEYING BAD NEWS WITH CONSIDERATE BUFFERS

On many business occasions, you will be able to buffer your delivery of bad news by helpful comments and explanations. For example, colleges tell many scholarship applicants the bad news of "no money" using this type of buffer:

> *"This year State University received more than 4,700 applications for the 800 tuition scholarships available. Because of such limited funding, many highly qualified applicants did not receive scholarship aid."*

The letter goes on to deliver the bad news regarding the reader's application and to offer alternative sources for college support.

A Silicon Valley computer company regularly uses this buffer to begin bad news letters to unsuccessful job applicants:

> *"We deeply appreciate your interest in employment at XYZ Corporation. At present, we do not have career openings suitable for your qualifications."*

The letter goes on to say that application materials will be kept on file for a period of one year. Introductory buffers should be informational or complimentary in tone, but never so rosy in tone as to arouse false expectations for the reader. A job applicant, for example, shouldn't be teased with the opening sentence, "Your qualifications are ideal!" if the next sentence conveys the bad news that the job went to someone else.

Here are four useful buffers for a variety of bad news communications.

1. This buffer helps the candidate understand why he or she was not chosen:

> *The company limited its search to candidates with LISP and COBOL programming experience.*

2. This buffer helps late applicants understand why their bids were unsuccessful:

> *The federal funding cycle required that we arrange subcontractors no later than April 1.*

3. This buffer helps candidates understand their chances:

> *Competition for these three positions was keen. More than 300 applications were received.*

4. This buffer helps an employee feel that his or her contribution was not ignored, even though a raise wasn't forthcoming:

> *Our decisions on merit raises this year were made extremely difficult by the limited funds available. Not all meritorious employees could be recognized by raises.*

CONVEYING BAD NEWS WITHOUT EXTENSIVE EXPLANATION

At times, you may not want or be able to provide cogent justification or explanation for the bad news you deliver. In credit refusals, for example, you may risk libel action by attempting to specify exactly why credit was denied. Compare, for example, the hazardous explanations in the "before" letter with the safe, brief "no" communication in the "after" version.

Before revision:

Dear Mr. Reynolds:

Your application for credit cannot be approved at this time because of substantial unpaid balances on three credit cards; lingering credit problems due to your recent divorce; disputed billings with two department stores; and a low rating of 2 on our measurement scale of employment stability.

This kind of letter is sure to draw an angry response and perhaps a legal challenge from the reader.

After revision:

> *Dear Mr. Reynolds:*
>
> *Thank you for applying for credit with XYZ Company. We regret that we cannot extend the credit you request at this time. If you have questions about your credit record you may contact TRW Credit Services at 555-3892 within 60 days of this letter for a copy of your credit report without charge.*

Similarly, you may not choose to cite chapter-and-verse reasons for bad news responses to many requests and invitations.

> *Dear Ms. Collins:*
>
> *I'm sorry I won't be able to accept your kind invitation to present the keynote address for this year's Community Fund convention.*
>
> *Thank you for thinking of me, and my very best wishes for the success of your meeting.*

This kind of direct, polite refusal is preferable to the white lies that so often accompany "no" messages. The writer could have told Ms. Collins, contrary to fact, that he had to be out of town on the convention weekend. If it is later discovered (as it may be) that he has lied, both he and Ms. Collins will feel the awkwardness of the situation. Besides, whether he's caught or not, it's both wrong and unnecessary to lie.

Here's another example of a bad news message without extended explanation, this time in memo form.

To: Virginia Flores
     Human Services

From: Brenda Nathanson
       Vice President

Subject: Additional Staff

Virginia, I gave careful attention to your well-reasoned request for two additional secretaries. Unfortunately, the budget won't allow me to say yes this year.

Let's get together if you would like to talk about ways to deal with your work load under present staffing limits. I won't forget your request, by the way, when fiscal pressures ease up.

Notice in this memo that the vice president does not choose to give her employee a detailed justification for her decision. The decision is "no," though delivered politely and with the offer of help.

Especially in decisions regarding new product development, regulatory problems, taxation, personnel, compensation, hiring, and policy, business leaders often find that less is more—the less said, the better. This guideline should not be taken as a license for managers to deny information to clients, employees, and the public. But managers should not always feel obligated to supply complete rationales for every "no" decision. The pace and nature of daily business life often make such disclosure both impractical and inadvisable.

TEN SELF-COACHING REMINDERS WHEN YOU MUST SAY "NO"

◆ I am saying "no" to ideas, requests, or invitations, not to the person.

◆ My job requires me to say "no" at times. It's not personal.

◆ Hearing "no" from me is hardly the end of the world for the other person.

◆ I can offer alternatives along with my "no" answer, but I'm not obligated to do so.

◆ "No" can be said in a friendly way that shows respect and liking for the other person.

◆ My "no" answer can often be understood and accepted by the other person if I let them see the issue from my point of view.

◆ If I need to say "no" but waffle with ambiguous answers, I am losing my own credibility with the other person and increasing their eventual disappointment.

◆ By choosing the right time and place to say "no" I can minimize emotional blowups on the part of the disappointed person.

◆ Whenever I say "no," I also need to communicate that my door remains open for other ideas and requests in the future.

◆ I should accompany my "no" answer with an apology only when I have something to apologize for. An empty apology is insincere. If I need to say more about my "no" answer, I can choose to explain rather than to apologize.

BAD NEWS RESPONSES TO CLAIMS

Contrary to the old saying, customers aren't always right. Often they make claims upon the company that cannot and should not be granted.

Take the case of an Ohio bus company. It purchased three commuter-size buses from the manufacturer, Regent Coaches. Within a year, the cloth upholstery in all three buses was showing significant wear. The bus company wrote to the manufacturer to demand that all seat covers be replaced in a more durable material without expense to the purchaser.

From the perspective of the manufacturer, this claim can't be granted. First, seat coverings—along with wiper blades, batteries, and headlight bulbs—are explicitly exempted from warranties on the buses in question. Second, the purchaser selected the least expensive seat-cover fabric (identified in writing by the manufacturer at the time of sale as suitable for "light use" only) even though the buses received heavy daily use.

If possible, the bad news to the purchaser must be delivered in a constructive, nonadversarial way. The manufacturer doesn't want to drive former customers away. For this reason, the following letter suggests options that help the purchaser resolve the seat-cover problem without compromising the warranty standards and policies of the manufacturer.

◆

Dear Mr. Green:

Thank you for your careful description in your May 1 letter of wear-and-tear problems with seat coverings in your Regent buses. Although fabric repairs are exempted from the bus warranty (see paragraph 9), let me suggest a long-term solution to the problem you describe.

The success of your bus routes is amply demonstrated by your number of passengers per day—heavy use you may not have anticipated when you selected fabric for your bus seats. To plan for continued heavy use in the future, you should consider installing DurEver coverings, which do carry a five-year guarantee against tears, fraying, or surface wear.

We can arrange to have these coverings installed on an overnight basis at your site. Costs for your three Regent buses are enclosed on a separate estimate form. Please note that the cost of this upgrade is far less over five years than the two or more sets of cloth seat fabrics you could expect to install in that period.

I'll call you within the next few days to discuss your seat-cover options. Or, if you wish, give me a call at 555-3902.

Sincerely

Corey L. Watkins

Corey L. Watkins
Service Manager

◆

Will the customer not only swallow the bad news that he isn't getting new seat covers, but also come back to the manufacturer with a new order? Time will tell. But the sales manager has given this situation his best effort by *a*) delivering the bad news honestly, *b*) suggesting workable alternatives, and *c*) treating the customer with respect. One thing is for sure: a flat turndown—"No, you're not getting a thing from us beyond your warranty"—would have soured business relations permanently.

Although employees do not usually write claim memos to the company, they do send forward complaints in various forms. A manager's bad news response to a complaint about work conditions is on the next page. Notice in this response that the manager dignifies the complaint, not belittles it; conveys the bad news respectfully, not vindictively; and concludes with a statement of goodwill, not peevishness.

Sure, it's a small thing—one employee was too hot, and decided to write the big boss about it. But employer-employee relations are built up, for better or worse, by such small encounters. In this case, the manager took a few minutes to check into the situation and to say "no" to the employee's request for cooler temperatures. The bad news was delivered tactfully, however, with room left open for further discussion.

The manager could have chosen to belittle the complainer—"Bill, you're the only person who thinks the office is too hot"—or ridicule the complaint—"you seem to think I have nothing else to worry about besides the air conditioning thermostat!" Wisely, however, the manager listens to the complaint, makes a decision, and communicates it respectfully.

July 3, 20__

    To: William Tolson
          Marketing

  From: Ellen Rogers
          Director, Marketing and Sales

 Subject: Your Concerns about Work Environment Temperatures

Bill, I understand from your memo of July 1 that you feel your work area is too warm during sunny afternoons. You requested any data I have on this matter and ask that I take action.

Here's my follow up. The Climate Engineering office tells me that room temperatures in your area are between 78 and 80 degrees during even the warmest summer days. Under our agreement with the Environmental Protection Agency for energy savings, the company has committed not to turn down air conditioning below these temperature levels during the summer.

I hope you'll let me know immediately if room temperatures rise above the 80 degree limit. If you feel we need to work out some special arrangement for your continued work efficiency, please contact my secretary so we can find time to meet.

SUMMARY KEYS TO DELIVERING BAD NEWS MESSAGES

1. Use buffers to take the emotional edge off bad news that you know will disappoint or anger the message recipient.

2. Include an explanation for your "no" decision when circumstances allow. Do not feel obligated to justify every "no" decision.

3. Explanations given for "no" decisions should be truthful and nonmanipulative.

Chapter 6

Here's a Mixed Bag:

Good News and Bad News

◆

A mixed bag message . . . should aim for one predominant effect upon the reader.

This chapter shows how to write business messages that contain a variety of messages, perhaps including both good news and bad news. But such messages should not turn into shopping bags stuffed with many items in no particular order. As we will see, the mixed bag message must have a purposeful design to accomplish its communication goals.

Many letters and memos in daily business include both good and bad news. You write to tell your salespeople that their commission rates have been increased, but their territories decreased in size. You write to tell customers that their orders will be shipped, but not at your expense, as the customers had requested.

At such time, what goes where? Should good news always come before bad, or vice versa? Should you create a good news sandwich, with a slab of bad news in the middle? And how do you make smooth transitions between good news and bad? ("And now for something entirely different . . .")

These are the kinds of dilemmas that make mixed bag messages some of the most poorly written (and, therefore, most dangerous) communications in business. This chapter doesn't offer blanket answers; the placement of good and bad news in a letter or memo depends upon your purpose, your reader, and the circumstances.

Instead we emphasize one guiding principle: A mixed bag message, though composed of contrasting parts, is one communication and should aim for one predominant effect upon the reader.

MIXED RESPONSES TO ORDERS, INQUIRIES, AND REQUESTS

Put yourself in the shoes of a customer. You placed an urgent order, and now you receive a confirming letter. Would you prefer to read the good news first—that the company can fill the order—or the bad news—that it will arrive a few days after your big sale?

For the writer, the key here is not so much the arrangement of good and bad news as the connection between the two. Notice in these before and after versions how the proper connection between good and bad news makes all the difference to the customer.

Before version:

> *Dear Mr. Herbert:*
>
> *Thank you for your order #2983 received January 11, 20__. Be assured that it will be filled carefully and completely, and shipped to you via UPS overnight service as you requested.*
>
> *Because of assembly delays, we will not be able to fill the entire order until Feb. 1. We trust this delay does not inconvenience you.*
>
> *We appreciate your business and look forward to serving you in the future.*

After reading this letter, the customer wails, "Those idiots! I don't even want the order if it can't get here by January 25th for my sale. I told them to deliver by the 25th!" In the "after" version, the proper connection between good news and bad news prevents such apoplexy on the customer's part, and probably saves the sale.

After revision:

> *Dear Mr. Herbert:*
>
> *We're eager to fill your order #2983 received January 11, 20__. But first we want to make sure that our shipping schedule meets your needs.*
>
> *Because of assembly delays, we will be able to ship 60 percent of your order to arrive by January 25, and the balance to arrive Feb. 1, both by UPS overnight. Will 60 percent of the total order be*

> *sufficient for the sale period you describe in your letter?*
>
> *Please contact us as soon as possible by fax (555-2903) or phone (555-9939) regarding your wishes. We appreciate your order and want to fill it to your satisfaction.*

In this "after" version, the customer recognizes from the beginning that the company understands the situation.

When responding to requests and invitations, you must be the judge (based on your purpose, audience, and circumstance) whether good news should precede or follow bad news in a mixed bag message. Here are examples of each arrangement for both requests (memo form) and invitations (letter form).

May 11, 20___

    To: Lisa Reardon
         Product Development

From: Barbara Walsh
         Vice President

Subject: Your Request for Additional Computing Resources

I have approved your request for six additional computing stations for Seventh Floor operations.

However, I think we can save money by purchasing six "dumb" terminals linked to a single file-server rather than acquiring six stand-alone PCs, as you requested. My approval, therefore, is contingent on your acceptance of this change.

I've passed along the purchase authorization to Lee Harvest (ext. 2983). Please contact him if you're ready to proceed, or give me a call if you have questions or concerns (ext. 8923).

Here is an alternate way of presenting the preceding message, with bad news first:

I think we can save money, Lisa, by purchasing "dumb" terminals linked to a single file-server rather than the six stand-alone PCs you request.

With this change, I have sent along an approved purchase authorization for the equipment to Lee Harvest (ext. 2983). Please contact him if you're ready to proceed, or give me a call if you have questions or concerns (ext. 8923).

Which version is best? The answer to that question depends upon your knowledge of Lisa Reardon, your reader. If Lisa will be pleased enough by your approval to swallow your rather high-handed change in her order, then put the good news first. But if you think Lisa prefers to tie up loose ends before moving ahead, present the bad news regarding your change before the good news of your approval.

Here are alternate versions of a mixed bag response to an invitation.

Dear Mr. Billings:

It will give me genuine pleasure to speak to your Rotary Club on Feb. 8 regarding my years as a research scientist for the Navy.

Unfortunately, I won't be able to speak, as you request, about developments in the SO4 atomic submarine program. Design and performance aspects of that project are classified.

I'm sure, however, that we can settle upon another topic of interest to your members. Please give me a call (555-3892) so that we can make arrangements.

With best regards,

Samuel R. Benton

Samuel R. Benton, Ph.D.

◆

Notice in this letter the writer's confidence that the Rotary Club wants him for a speaker, whether or not he can talk on the requested topic. In an alternate version, the writer leaves open the possibility that the group may only want him to speak on the submarine project or not at all:

> *Thanks for your kind invitation to speak to the Rotary Club on Feb. 8. Unfortunately, the topic you suggest—SO4 submarine developments—is still classified.*
>
> *I am available to speak on this date, however, on other topics related to naval research. Please give me a call (555-3892) so we can discuss the interests of your group.*

MIXED BAG MESSAGES IN CREDIT COMMUNICATIONS

Letters and memos granting credit are usually made up not only of the good news—you've got credit—but also a laundry list of terms and conditions that, read closely, may constitute mild bad news.

As a general rule, place the good news of credit approval by itself at the beginning of the message. Give the reader at least this brief moment to bask in the satisfaction of being a potential debtor. Then, in the later paragraphs, spell out the various restrictions, limitations, and other contractual realities affecting the credit line.

> *Dear Ms. Owens:*
>
> *Kendall Wholesale Supply is pleased to grant your request for a retailer's credit line in the amount of $25,000.*
>
> *As described in the accompanying credit disclosure brochure, interest at a rate of 18 percent per*

annum will be charged on unpaid balances exceeding 30 days. No interest is charged if payment is received within 30 days.

Signators to the credit purchasing plan are limited to those listed on page 2 of your application form. The company reserves the right to approve any additional signators.

On behalf of our 286 employees, I'm happy to welcome you to the group of more than 3,800 retailers now served by Kendall Wholesale Supply.

But if your credit-related message is predominantly negative, place the bad news first, after an appropriate buffer:

Dear Ms. Owens:

Thank you for contacting us regarding credit purchasing. At present, we are not able to open a credit line in the amount you request. (You can review your credit file without charge by calling Dun & Bradstreet, 555-3892, within 60 days of receiving this letter.)

Many of our most established customers prefer to take advantage of the 5 percent cash discount offered by Kendall Wholesale Supply. The enclosed catalog describes both the discount program (p. 7) and our spring line.

We hope to serve your needs in the near future.

MIXED BAG MESSAGES IN RESPONSES TO COMPLAINTS AND CLAIMS

Customer service representatives and others who do business with the public would have easier lives if messages sent to these audiences said simply, "yes, your claim is granted," or "no, get lost."

In the real world, however, many communications to customers and public stakeholders are mixed messages. The placement of good news and bad news depends on the now-familiar "big three": your purpose, your reader, and the circumstance.

If, for example, your goal is to clear up your reader's misunderstandings or educate him or her on proper procedures, you may choose to place your good news toward the end of the letter or memo. In this way, you hold the reader's attention. (After the good news, the reader may have little motive to read on.)

In the following memo, a manager makes clear to an employee that proper channels weren't used (the bad news) even though the employee's complaint will be resolved (the good news).

February 6, 20__

   To: Morton Fairley
         Accounting

  From: Hanna Roth
         Accounting Supervisor

 Subject: Resolving Your Lighting Problems

I was surprised to hear from Bob Foster, our division manager, that you had written to him regarding flickering and buzzing light fixtures in your office. Mr. Foster has asked me to look into the matter.

As a matter of common practice, Morton, you should contact your work unit leader or me about such items. When a message goes forward directly to Mr. Foster, he can't help but assume that you've already tried (and failed) to get help from your immediate supervisors.

As for the problem itself, I've contacted Building Repair (as you could have—extension 982) and the problem will be resolved by Friday. Let me know if you have concerns about this or other aspects of your work environment.

◆

And in the next letter, a customer service representative educates a customer about warranty terms before compromising (the good news) to make the problem go away.

Dear Mr. Williams:

I understand from the homeware department head (Linda King) at our Cambridge store that you returned an air conditioner to her department and asked for a complete refund. According to Ms. King, you presented a receipt showing that you bought the air conditioner from our store 18 months ago (July 7, 20__). She has referred the matter to me for resolution.

The warranty accompanying your air conditioner provides for one year parts and labor service. It is the policy of this company to offer a complete refund for a one-year period from date of purchase. Since you purchased your air conditioner 18 months ago, neither the warranty nor the refund policy any longer applies.

Nevertheless, we are eager to see you satisfied with your purchase. The manufacturer has authorized me to extend your warranty period for one additional month, during which time the air conditioner will be repaired without expense to you.

If this plan meets with your approval, please call Ms. King (555–3892) at your earliest convenience to arrange for repairs.

Sincerely,

Alice Roper
Customer Service

SUMMARY KEYS IN WRITING MIXED BAG MESSAGES

1. Decide where to place good news and bad news according to your purpose, your reader, and your circumstances.

2. Delay bad news if your reader won't read beyond it to the good news.

3. Delay good news if your reader won't read beyond it to neutral information or necessary bad news.

Chapter 7

The Extended Letter:

Reports and Proposals

◆

Letter or memo reports and proposals are usually less than five pages long.

This chapter shows how to package complicated, extended messages into document formats that remain readable and interesting. For the writer, the process of condensing a substantial amount of material into a limited space takes hard thinking and skilled wordsmithing. The payoff for such work lies in the gratitude of readers who grasp your points easily and are therefore more likely to be persuaded to your perspective or recommended action.

Let's say that you face a choice: you can read a ten-page report or a two-page condensation of the same report in memo form. Which would you choose?

If your in-basket resembles a paper blizzard, you'll probably opt for the shorter form. So do most managers across industries. Like you, these men and women face more and more words to read each day, thanks to modern "time-savers" such as word processing, high-speed printing, high-tech photocopying, and electronic mail. When it comes to business documents, most professionals would agree "the shorter the better."

This chapter discusses how to use letter and memo formats to write brief reports and proposals. In doing so, the writer maintains two features of the conventional letter or memo:

◆ the layout (block, modified block, or simplified for letters, or memo format)

◆ the conversational style, particularly in the first paragraph of the letter or memo

In addition, three features are borrowed from traditional reports and proposals:

◆ headings (and, for longer documents, subheadings)

◆ graphs, charts, and tables as required

◆ in-text complete citation of sources. (Letter or memo reports and proposals rarely include a section of Works Cited, endnotes, or footnotes.)

Reports and proposals in letter or memo form are usually less than five pages long.

THE USES OF LETTER AND MEMO REPORTS

The letter form is used to report to out-of-company audiences, including clients, regulators, community representatives, shareholders, and others. The memo form is used to report to in-house audiences, including various levels of management and other departments.

The letter and memo report is commonly used for:

◆ problem assessments and analyses

◆ trip reporting

◆ laboratory and test recording

◆ procedural and policy reports

◆ feasibility studies

◆ progress reporting

◆ periodic reporting

THE LOGIC OF LETTER AND MEMO REPORTS

No matter what the use, most letter and memo reports follow a similar developmental pattern:

Opening (first paragraph) Conversational statement of purpose for the ensuing material.

Topic or Problem Statement (second paragraph) Specific description of the topic or problem under discussion.

Necessary Background (third paragraph, or combined with second paragraph) A concise history of the topic or problem. No more background is given than is necessary for the reader to understand the material at hand.

Significant Developments (middle paragraphs, as required) Description and/or analysis of current action or thinking with regard to the topic or problem.

Assessment (middle paragraphs, as required) An evaluation of what is working and what remains to be done.

Conclusion and Recommendations (final paragraphs) Summary statement of results, with specific recommendations for future action. (Note that the Conclusions and Recommendations section may also be placed at the beginning of the letter or memo report, following the Opening. In that case, the letter or memo report would conclude with a brief summary statement.)

Appropriate Well-wishing, Appreciation, and *Contact Information* (last sentences) Final thanks, if appropriate, to the reader and information on where questions and comments can be directed.

The Letter Report

Each of the categories above usually forms a section of the letter report set off by a heading (as illustrated in the following sample). Note that the headings are content-specific (that is, they include words that refer to the content of the report) and that Roman numerals are not used for headings. A subject line is often used to take the place of the title that would appear in traditional report formatting.

A SAMPLE LETTER REPORT

June 8, 20__

Ms. Helen Kent, Vice President
SuperBuy Grocery Markets, Inc.
92 Lester Road
Boston, MA 01829

Subject: Presentations at the Annual Managers Meeting

Dear Ms. Kent:

It was good to see you again at the National Food Industry Council meeting, and I was glad to hear about your recent promotion at SuperBuy. Congratulations! As you requested, I'm writing to offer ideas for making your annual meetings more effective.

Since our discussion, I have read participant evaluations from the last four SuperBuy managers meetings and have spoken with many managers and senior executives in your company. In general, these sources judge the annual meetings to be an unproductive use of time—"boring," "repetitive," "just a lot of talking," and "amateurish" are recurring descriptions. My report assesses the information provided by these sources and offers recommendations for more effective annual meetings.

A Brief History of the Annual Managers Meeting

SuperBuy began holding annual managers meetings in 1995. The first five meetings (1995–1999) were organized and run by a professional meeting planner, who brought in several "name" presenters. Attendees simply sat back and watched the show.

As costs for such services rose, however, SuperBuy's CEO (Eric Wetherspoon) decided to use in-house talent in place of paid presenters. Through 2001, Wetherspoon and other top executives themselves made the major presentations at the annual meeting. This practice ended abruptly after a 2001 survey showed that 85 percent of managers attending the meeting found these executive briefings to be uninspiring, redundant, and poorly prepared.

For the 2002 meeting, the company's new CEO (Sheila Morgan) selected rank-and-file managers as speakers for the meeting. Over a period of two days, a total of ten one-hour speeches was delivered by ten managers at that meeting. Response from participants was highly favorable. Although the presentations were far from professional, they dealt with down-to-earth issues in terms that managers understood. This format for meeting speakers has continued to the present.

Current Controversy and Complaints Among Speakers

A few days after the 2003 annual managers meeting, the CEO received a letter of complaint signed by all ten managers/speakers for that meeting. The letter pointed out that "we are not trained professional speakers, and therefore should not be asked to make presentations before large audiences unless we also receive adequate training to do so. For many of us, the process of developing a presentation and delivering it was a professional nightmare that included serious bouts with speaker's nerves, dozens of uncompensated hours of preparation in addition to our usual duties, and little assistance from the company in the preparation of necessary slides and other visual aids."

Based on this letter and subsequent meetings with these speakers, the CEO has decided to make as-yet undefined changes in how speakers are selected for next year's meeting.

Evaluation of Speakers' and Participants' Responses

All parties to the annual meeting (including the CEO, top management, the speakers, and participating managers) seem to agree on two points:

1. In-house speakers are preferable to out-of-house speakers.

2. Managers are preferable as speakers to top management.

In addition, most meeting attendees have been favorably impressed by the managers' speeches, even though the speakers themselves felt their efforts to be somewhat amateurish.

The key point, however, is the stress described by managers who are selected to give speeches. Many have been so terrified by the idea of speaking before an audience of 1,000 or more that they sought professional counseling and medical aid to get them through the experience. Others say that they have considered quitting their jobs because of the burden of speech preparation and delivery.

The solution to these problems, according to the presenting managers, lies in adequate speech coaching and company assistance in preparing visual aids.

Conclusion and Recommendations

In summary, the company is at an impasse: the CEO wants managers to speak, but they resist doing so without support from the company in the form of speech coaching and assistance in producing visual aids.

Since the company saves more than $50,000 each meeting by not employing outside professional speakers, a small portion of those funds (perhaps $5,000 to $10,000) should be devoted to expert speech coaching for the selected managers. An additional amount (perhaps $3,000–$4,000) can be spent on the production of professional visual aids.

Recommendations:

1. Interview and retain a speech consultant to work closely with selected managers in the preparation of their material and development of their delivery skills.

2. Determine whether in-house audiovisual services can provide support in the production of visual aids for speakers. If not, an outside firm should be retained for this purpose.

3. Survey the responses of speakers and attendees at this year's meeting to assess the effectiveness of speech coaching and visual aid assistance.

I recognize, Helen, that this matter has fallen in your lap as one of your new job responsibilities. Don't hesitate to call me to discuss any of these ideas. I would also be glad to suggest a list of reputable speech consultants in your area.

Good luck with your planning for this year's meeting, and best personal regards.

Cordially,

Robert R. Henderson

Robert R. Henderson
Director
Food Industry Institute

◆

If Henderson worked within the SuperBuy organization, this same information could have been cast in the form of a memo report, using the typical To: From: Subject: headings.

The Memo Report

In the following example, the memo format has been used for a trip report. Note that the elements of topic statement, background, developments, assessment, and conclusion/recommendations are still present, although named in content-specific language in the headings.

April 14, 20__

   To: Roger Wilson
        Manager

 From: Forest Thompson
        Sales Associate

 Subject: Results of Business Trip to Miami area, April 4–9, 20__.

We already discussed by phone some of the results of my Miami trip, Roger, but I want to sum up matters in a complete way with this memo.

Assigned Travel

From April 4–9, I visited four companies in the greater Miami area: Likert Mills, Brenton Carpets, Western Fabric Supply, and Anderson Home Systems. Each of these firms wholesales more than $15 million of residential and commercial carpeting each year. The purpose of my sales call was to assess their use of stain-blocking treatments and to promote our new product, STAINGUARD.

Background

Until 1998, none of these companies pretreated its carpeting with a stain-blocker. Two of the companies (Brenton and Anderson) sold an after-installation spot remover comparable to commercially available sprays such as Spot-Out and Sani-Clean.

With the growing use of stain-blocking nylon fibers beginning in 1998, all four companies began searching for ways to pretreat all their carpets, including nylons and nylon blends, with some cost-effective stain-blocker. Market research demonstrated the attractiveness of the "stain-blocker" concept for retail purchasers.

Likert and Western developed their own in-house treatments, while Brenton and Anderson experimented with a chemical treatment originally intended for odor removal. To date, none of the companies reports satisfaction with their chosen processes.

Nature of Sales Calls

At extended meetings with company decision makers at each firm, I demonstrated the STAINGUARD product and pointed out independent laboratory evaluations of its effectiveness. Using samples of their own carpeting, I showed the efficacy of STAIN-GUARD treatment to prevent staining by wine, sodas, fruit juices, food residues, and common inks.

Following this demonstration, I explained how STAINGUARD can be applied as an easy step in the carpet manufacturing process. Together with their accounting personnel, I calculated approximate costs per yard for the STAINGUARD difference.

Assessment of Customer Responses
My demonstrations were received very favorably at all four companies. Executives at Brenton and Western seemed especially impressed by the cost savings accrued through the use of STAINGUARD when compared to their present stain-prevention treatment. Management at Likert and Anderson requested phone numbers of companies now using STAINGUARD, and I provided these references.

Conclusion and Recommendations
I felt that the Miami trip was worthwhile in promoting STAIN-GUARD to four well-known carpet manufacturers. Use of our product by any one of them would attract significant interest by other carpet manufacturers throughout the area.

To lead these four companies from interest to actual purchase, our technical staff must be prepared to give them specific guidance on how the STAINGUARD step can best be integrated into their present manufacturing process.

Recommendations:

1. Authorize our technical staff to prepare preliminary installation descriptions of STAINGUARD equipment for each manufacturer.

2. Authorize return travel to the Miami area in mid-May for me and a technical representative. On this trip we will present installation suggestions and, I'm confident, bring back significant orders.

If you have questions or comments, Roger, give me a call (ext. 198). I'll be in the office all this week.

◆

EIGHT WAYS TO IMPROVE YOUR WRITING

Building anything—including an effective communication—involves progressive stages. Leaping ahead to install windows and doors can be disastrous if you haven't yet ensured a solid foundation and strong walls for your structure. Documents grow to their final form by similarly logical stages:

◆ *Stage 1 Grasp your purpose* What do you want to achieve?

◆ *Stage 2 Analyze your audience* To whom are you speaking? What do they expect from you? What is their background? What kind of terms, examples, and details can you use to best effect?

◆ *Stage 3 Brainstorm* How can your topic be best developed for your audience? What aspects of your topic will be most interesting? What examples will best support your points?

◆ *Stage 4 Limit your material* Out of all the ideas stirred up during brainstorming, what ideas are most appropriate for your purpose and audience? What ideas can you write about with the most expertise and confidence?

◆ *Stage 5 Organize your material* What logical pattern can be used to communicate your ideas clearly and persuasively? In what order should your ideas appear?

◆ *Stage 6 Substantiate your points* Before beginning to draft your document, "plug in" appropriate support passages, including examples, details, anecdotes, and statistics. Locate places in your document where graphic aids, if needed, can be placed.

◆ *Stage 7 Draft your document* As if speaking to an interested friend, write out your argument from start to finish. Use natural words, short sentences, and short paragraphs.

◆ *Stage 8 Polish your document* Pay close attention to all matters of style, grammar, mechanics, spelling, and format to create a professional document that reflects well on you and your company.

◆

LETTER AND MEMO PROPOSALS

Proposals are similar to reports in that they both begin by addressing a particular problem or topic, giving background information, and evaluating current developments. The proposal differs from the report, however, in providing specific details about a plan of action to achieve particular goals. For example, a report on inadequate electrical service to a plant might focus on the problem and recommend that money be budgeted to repair the problem. A proposal on the same topic would also focus on the problem, but would go on to propose a specific plan (including information about equipment, personnel, facilities, and expenditures) to resolve the problem.

Letter and memo proposals are often written by contractors. If the proposal is accepted, a formal contract authorizing work will be signed.

The Letter Proposal

In the following letter proposal, an office design firm proposes to remodel an office on the accounting floor of a major corporation. The purpose of this proposal is to obtain authorization in concept for work proposed. Specific renderings of space usage and proposed furnishings will be provided by the contractor after the initial proposal has been accepted. (In this way, contractors avoid "spinning their wheels"—performing expensive planning work on behalf of companies who haven't yet decided to become clients.)

March 19, 20__

Mr. Ted Ainsworth
Managing Partner
Western Cities Architectural Design, Inc.
892 Star Drive
San Francisco, CA 98232

Subject: Proposal for Redesign of Accounting Wing

Dear Mr. Ainsworth:

I want to thank you and your executive committee for meeting with Lisa Johnson and me last Thursday. We are delighted that you like our preliminary suggestions for cost-effective remodeling of your accounting facilities.

In this letter, I want to sum up our discussions so far and propose the next steps in seeing this project on its way to reality.

Project Background

During the past decade, almost every sector of your Star Drive headquarters has been remodeled for the efficient and attractive use of space. Only the accounting area (sixth floor) still maintains its 1980s-ish bureaucratic look: desks in straight rows without separating partitions, outmoded lighting, unattractive wall coverings and decor, and brown vinyl flooring.

Due in large part to such unattractive work surroundings, your company has had trouble attracting and retaining qualified accounting personnel. Data from hiring interviews and exit interviews confirm the consensus among accounting personnel that their work area, in the words of a former accounting employee, "looks like and feels like a mental morgue."

Current Project Status

The accounting department traditionally experiences a slow period in their work requirements in the weeks following tax season (ending April 15). During these weeks, it will be possible to move accounting personnel to temporary quarters on the fourth floor.

Assuming that the proposed remodeling can be completed within 30 days from initiation shortly after April 15, the accounting department can be up and running again on the sixth floor by mid-May.

Proposed Specifics

Office Design, Inc., proposes a modular reorganization of the sixth floor office space, as depicted in Elevation A (attached). In this design, each accountant would work within his or her own space defined by partitions and planted areas. Wide corridors between such spaces will maintain the open feel of the area as well as easy physical access to work spaces.

State-of-the-art furniture (see attached List of Recommended Furniture) has been chosen to complement a harmonious room design while at the same time supporting the work needs of accountants. The model #792 desk, for example, makes special provision for a desktop PC, drawers for hard copy spreadsheets, and security drawers for proprietary and sensitive documents.

Remodeling will be undertaken in five stages:

> *Stage One* April 18–23 Removal of existing furnishings, wall and floor coverings.
> *Stage Two* April 24–30 Surface preparation of walls and floors for new coverings.

> *Stage Three* May 1–5 Installation of diaphragm lighting system.
>
> *Stage Four* May 6–10 Installation of new wall and floor coverings.
>
> *Stage Five* May 11–14 Installation of office furniture and plants.

Western Cities Architectural Design will not be required to supply any personnel, including janitorial staff, for purposes of this work. All workers performing labor for Office Design, Inc., will be bonded and insured. It will be the responsibility of Office Design, Inc., to obtain all necessary permits and inspections for the proposed work.

Schedule of Fees
Payment for the proposed work is requested in three installments:

1. $145,000 retainer upon acceptance of this proposal

2. $150,000 at the completion of Stage Three

3. $150,000 at the completion of Stage Five and project sign-off by City inspectors.

Total consideration: $445,000.

Conclusion
We invite your close attention to the renderings and furniture brochures accompanying this proposal. As you review these materials, please feel free to call upon us with any questions or concerns. If you approve this project proposal, our legal counsel can meet with yours to draw up mutually acceptable contracts reflecting the terms described above.

Thank you for considering the services of Office Design, Inc. We look forward to working with you.

Sincerely

Ellen O. Wilson

Ellen O. Wilson
Vice President

◆

The Memo Proposal

Good ideas spawned within a business organization often die because no one takes the time to commit them to paper in the form of a memo proposal. No matter how appealing the idea, it usually cannot be passed along to higher levels of review and approval in verbal form. Someone has to write it down.

In the following memo proposal, a midlevel manager describes a better way to control absenteeism. Many companies award bonuses for employee ideas that lead to better work efficiency or morale.

◆

January 11, 20__

    To: Patricia R. Roberts
          Operations Vice President

  From: James Long
           Manager, Division 6

Subject: A Plan for Significant Reductions in Employee Absenteeism

In your general memo of Dec. 10, you invite company employees to write up ideas that may save the company money and improve the work environment. I appreciate your consideration of my proposal for a sick family member facility here at our headquarters to reduce employee absenteeism.

Background of the Absenteeism Problem

In my division, a total of 212 employees took 1,418 sick days during the last fiscal year. The expense to the company in lost labor was approximately $260,500. If that same ratio is true for the company's 750 other employees, then the company is losing more than $1 million per year to sick days.

I conducted a survey of these employees to determine, on an anonymous basis, whether their sick time was in fact being used because of their own illness or because of that of family members, including children and elderly parents.

Of the 160 survey forms returned, 46 percent of the employees said that at least half their sick days were taken not for themselves but for family members in their care. In the vast majority of these cases, the illnesses involved were neither serious nor long-lasting: colds, flu, stomach upsets, and so forth.

Company Options

As the number of elderly increases in our society and the number of children per family begins to rise again (after a 20-year decline), we can expect our employees to be taking even more sick time for the care of these family members.

Or the company can act in its own interest and that of its employees to establish a sick family member room coordinated with the company infirmary. Cost savings, as calculated below, would amount to at least $150,000 per year, with the additional advantage of improved employee morale and significant recruitment advantages.

Proposal Specifics

1. At present, Room D at the company health center is not used. I propose that it be furnished with four hospital beds and appropriate furnishings. Approximate cost: $15,000.

2. Two health officers (Dr. White and Nurse Evans) now maintain services at the company. I propose that a licensed practical nurse (LPN) be hired to assist them in the additional care required for Room D patients. Approximate cost: $65,000 per year.

3. Finally, I propose that the Executive Committee work together with Dr. White and Nurse Evans to define standards for admittance to the health center.

If the availability of a sick family member room were publicized to employees, the company stands to save hundreds of thousands of dollars. Precise calculations can be made at such times as final costs are determined for setup of the facility and employee use patterns become apparent.

Conclusion

I urge you to consider this low-cost and practical plan to reduce absenteeism. If I can be helpful in further employee surveys or other aspects of this project, please call on me.

SUMMARY KEYS FOR THE
EXTENDED LETTER OR MEMO

1. Extended documents that contain a variety of materials should nevertheless aim for one predominant effect or purpose.

2. A logical plan is crucial for extended documents. Readers must be aware of this logical path at all times as they read long messages.

3. Headings and subheadings act as signposts to guide the mental journey of the reader through an extended document.

Chapter 8

◆

Writing a Great Short Report:

Making and Supporting Your Point

Short reports are used for making decisions.

This chapter shows how to meet the challenge of writing a short report for your organization. Like a playoff game in sports, the short report is a highly visible opportunity to demonstrate your skills for a larger audience. You have the chance to create intelligent arguments and influence the course of decision-making. Put simply, when you write a short report, you have the opportunity to score in your company.

WHAT'S A SHORT REPORT?

Short reports are usually less than ten pages in length and can be read in one sitting. Business organizations of all sizes rely on these documents to learn what's happening in two worlds:

◆ *The internal world* What are employees working on? How is it going? What resources are being used or which are required? In what ways is the company growing or shrinking? What problems need to be addressed?

◆ *The external world* How is the company perceived by clients and the general public? What do clients want from the company? What is the company's competition? How can it be met? How can the company attract skilled workers? What social responsibilities and political challenges does the company face?

These issues and others are discussed by means of all communication channels in the company, including meetings, interviews, memos, letters, and so forth. However, the short report often addresses these issues more thoroughly and definitely, and in a more formal way than other forms of business communication.

WHY WRITE SHORT REPORTS?

The purpose of a short report may be informative *(what* is known about the topic), analytical *(why* certain problems have developed), persuasive *(how* readers should respond), or portions of all three. Because short reports are used for making decisions, they include enough evidence to support the recommendations contained in the report. Although short reports can refer to other written work, they should not just be cover letters to relatively disorganized collections of facts and figures.

ORDER OF PAGES IN A SHORT REPORT

As shown in Figure 1, there are six common types of pages in short reports. All are illustrated in the short report example at the end of this chapter.

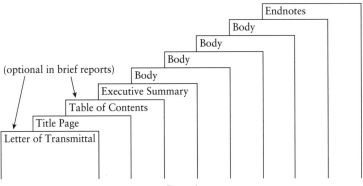

Figure 1

Letter of Transmittal   As shown in the sample report at the end of this chapter, this optional page is a letter from the report writer to the report reader. It briefly provides the following:

◆ reasons for the report

◆ authorization for writing the report

◆ highlights of particularly interesting aspects of the report

◆ contact information for reader's questions or comments

◆ statement of appreciation to those who assisted in the preparation of the report

Such letters usually appear in short reports that must be conveyed to their readers by mail or messenger rather than in person by the report writer. The letter of transmittal may also be attached to but not bound in with the report, in which case it does not appear in the table of contents. Pagination: count the letter of transmittal and number it in lowercase Roman numerals, if it's bound with the report.

Title Page   This page, the first the reader sees if a letter of transmittal is not included, contains key information: what the report is about (its title), for whom it was prepared, by whom it was written, and the date of its completion or filing. In addition, the title page is sometimes marked "Confidential" or "Proprietary" if its contents are particularly sensitive. Pagination: count the title page but show no Roman numeral page number.

Table of Contents   This page is optional in reports of six pages or less, but it is extremely helpful to readers of longer reports. Because your goal is to help readers understand your writing, include this element if it helps the reader. Don't include it if it only makes your report longer, not better. Pagination: count the table of contents and number it in lowercase Roman numerals, usually centered in the bottom margin. Do not enter "Table of Contents" as an item in your table of contents.

Executive Summary   This page may also be called an abstract or synopsis (more common in technical and scientific reports). It summarizes the purpose, organization, methods, and outcomes of the short report. The executive summary usually runs no longer than one page and may be as short as a single paragraph. Pagination: count the executive summary and number it in lowercase Roman numerals at the bottom of the page.

Report Body   These pages contain the actual information of the report, with major divisions of argument and evidence marked by headings. The development and organization of the report body is treated in depth later in this chapter. Pagination: the first page of the report body begins with Arabic number 1, continuing successively through all the remaining pages, including endnotes and bibliography, if any.

Endnotes, References, and Bibliography   Notes may be placed in the text itself, set at the foot of the page as footnotes, or gathered at the end of the report as endnotes. The references or bibliography pages, usually the last in a short report, always follow all notes and in-text references. Many short reports, of course, contain no notes and require no references or bibliography. Pagination: continue the sequence of Arabic numbers that began with the report body.

FIVE STEPS TO WRITING A GREAT SHORT REPORT

Professional report writers in business, industry, and government usually develop their own approaches to the craft of report writing. Some begin with wide reading in their topic area and extensive note taking. Others create an initial outline—a rough plan for the form and content of their eventual report—to guide their research efforts.

You, too, will develop your own approach to report writing. The five steps suggested here are a method used by many professional report writers. They may work well for you as well, or at least provide a place to start in your search for the most efficient way to write a great short report.

STEP ONE:
Think about the W-O-R-M

This acronym reminds you to review the basics before beginning to write:

W **Who** will read the report? What are the interests, needs, and biases of your readers? The answers to these questions help you determine what to discuss and how to shape your material to best effect.

O What is the **Object** of the report? What is your purpose in writing this report? Many professional report writers jot down their central purpose on a note card, which they keep in view while researching and writing. It's easy to get off track without this reminder.

R What is the **Range** of the report? With what breadth and depth should you treat your topic? Determining the range of your report inevitably means that you will have to leave out interesting but nonessential information.

M What is the **Method** of presentation in the report? Use topic headings, necessary graphics, tables, and white space to show the clear order of linked ideas in your report. Tell the reader early in the report how the report is organized.

STEP TWO:
Use the Classic Questions to brainstorm your topic

Perhaps the most common fault in report writing is beginning to write the actual words of the report too soon. Take time at the outset to think through your options for developing, presenting, and substantiating your ideas. To aid your brainstorming, use the following "Classic Questions" (so called because they have been used since the days of ancient Greece) to stimulate your thinking and turn up valuable ideas:

The Classic Questions

(Mentally fill in the blank in each question with your topic. Jot down notes when helpful ideas occur. Skip questions that don't apply well to your topic.)

1. Why do I/others even care about _____?

2. If I had to divide _____ into parts or stages, what would they be?

3. What forces/circumstances led to _____?

4. What kind of person is interested in _____?

5. If _____ did not exist, how would things be different?

6. What aspect of _____ do I (or would my readers) like best? Least?

7. What larger situation, cultural background, or other context helps to explain _____?

8. What are the principal benefits of _____?

9. If _____ fails or is ignored, what will be the impact? Upon whom?

10. How could _____ be explained to a 10-year-old child?

STEP THREE:

Develop a clear and persuasive pattern of argument

This is the step in which you "get your ducks in a row" by ordering and linking ideas into a meaningful, persuasive argument. This order of ideas should arise out of your analysis of audience, your grasp of purpose, and the nature of your topic. You can evaluate the order of your core ideas by placing them in an outline, as illustrated in Figure 2. This sample outline uses the common "past, present, future" order of organization.

I. *Overview*

   The purposes of the training program

   The key question: Is the company getting its money's worth?

II. *Past methods of training*

   What we used to do

   Why we did it that way

   How much it cost

III. *Present methods of training*

   What we do now

   Why we do it

   How much it costs

IV. *Evaluation*

   Old methods versus new methods

   Old costs versus new costs

V. *Conclusions*

   New costs are due to one-time equipment acquisition

   New methods are worth this expenditure

   Training per employee will cost less and less in the future

---

Figure 2

Although no one can invent an organizing pattern of ideas for you without knowing your audience, purpose, and topic, the following pattern of argument has also proved helpful as a starting place for shaping many short reports:

◆ *Section 1 Overview* (What will this report present? Why? What evidence was considered? What conclusions are justified?)

◆ *Section 2 Problem Definition and History* (What specific problem is addressed? What do we know about it? What is its history?)

◆ *Section 3 Problem Analysis and Impact* (Why is the problem occurring? Whom is it impacting? How?)

◆ *Section 4 Proposed Resolution* (How can the problem be solved? What reasons support this solution? What resources are necessary? What risks are involved? What benefits will accrue? To whom?)

◆ *Section 5 Action Recommendations* (What specific steps should be taken? By whom? When? Where?)

Conclude your work on organizing ideas by finding supporting details, examples, statistics, and anecdotes that help make your case. When you have accumulated these materials, you're ready to write the first draft of the report.

STEP FOUR:
Draft the report

Because you have taken the time to develop a working outline and a set of well-developed supporting details and examples, you may find the writing of the first draft surprisingly easy. You already know in general what you want to say. Somewhere in the back of your mind, the actual words of your draft may have begun to form during the outlining process. If first drafts have been excruciatingly hard for you to generate in the past, adopt a positive mindset for future writing: *I have prepared and can now express my ideas in a first draft without undue suffering.*

The trick to writing the first draft is to let go. Of course you will make mistakes along the way. You will no doubt wander at times and use unnecessary words. Nonetheless, let the words flow. You will discover what most professional report writers say: Quite a bit of the first draft turns out to be usable material in the final draft.

You may have to turn off internal editors and censors to write an effective first draft. There's the internalized voice, perhaps of a former English teacher, whispering, "Stop! Have you spelled correctly? Have you punctuated correctly?" There may be the voice of a parent or sibling: "That sounds awkward. Shouldn't you sound more intelligent?"

To all such voices, the effective writer says, "Wait." There is a time and place to edit and polish, but that time is not while you are writing the first draft. If you do your drafting at the computer, you know that changes can easily be made later. If you like to compose your first draft using pen and paper, make an effort to keep your writing instrument moving across the page, even if you have to draw a line to mark places where a particular word or phrase should occur but doesn't.

Another technique to try in the drafting process employs your considerable powers of conversation to motivate effective writing. Talk out a sentence or two before trying to write it. Once you have written for a while, read your work aloud. Try to continue the thoughts you've begun, just as if you were talking or writing to an interested friend. That natural, unaffected style will serve you well in business writing of all kinds.

STEP FIVE:
Revise and edit your draft

Finally, polish the rough diamond that lies on the desk before you so that others can appreciate it. Like your individual approach to writing the first draft, your revising and editing approach may differ from the following steps. However, if you have no systematic method for revision, you may want to practice these steps until they become second nature.

Check for Logical Connections

In the heat of argument, written or spoken, we may make logical errors. These can prove fatal to our writing if they appear in the final draft. Three logical errors in particular often surface in short reports:

Either/or thinking. *"Either this company buys new equipment or it faces a long and inevitable decline."* *(Are there really no other alternatives?)*

Circular reasoning. *"The sales manager's poor social skills prevented him from working successfully with people."* *(The second half of the sentence simply repeats the content of the first half of the sentence.)*

False cause. *"Johnson joined this company in 2003, and we've had nothing but problems since then."* *(It may be true that Johnson joined the company in 2003, and it may also be true that there have been nothing but problems since then. It does not necessarily follow that Johnson caused* the problems.)

Check for Appropriate Transitions

Readers should not feel an awkward mental lurch as you move from one sentence or paragraph to another. When your thoughts take a significant step forward, provide a bridge by using transitional words and phrases: *however, furthermore, therefore, similarly, in addition, although, for instance, increasingly, in effect,* and so on.

Eliminate Unnecessary Words

As you polish your rough draft, watch for "fat" words that contribute little or nothing to your message. Cut them out. Watch especially for repetitious language (*the unfounded misrepresentation*), meaningless phrases (*it is, there are*), and passages that wander from your point.

Test Your Diction for Power and Propriety

Diction is your choice of words. When reviewing your words, consider both their denotative (or dictionary meaning) and connotative meaning (emotional shading). The word *spinster*, for example, has the dictionary meaning of an unmarried female, but has the emotional content suggesting that the person lacks eligibility for marriage.

Check for Grammatical and Mechanical Errors

Slips in grammar and language mechanics can distract readers from your message. Readers may be justly suspicious, for example, of someone's claim to expertise as an "acountant" (notice the missing *c*). Use the Quick Guide to Grammar and Punctuation at the end of this book in completing a careful check of your draft.

Make Stylistic Improvements

As discussed throughout these chapters, your style of writing should fit the needs of your audience. For an in-house audience eager to grasp the point of your report as quickly as possible, use plain language, short sentences, and plenty of highlighting techniques such as bullets, headings, and boldface. For readers desiring a more formal or traditional presentation of information, use longer paragraphs, more elevated diction, and other techniques common to academic writing. The following checklist will guide your stylistic revisions:

◆ Use active verbs.

◆ Vary sentence types.

◆ Emphasize important words through placement.

◆ Be specific.

◆ Eliminate wordiness.

◆ Create parallels.

◆ Choose pronouns carefully.

◆ Control paragraph length.

◆ Avoid trite and slang expressions.

◆ Avoid contractions and abbreviations.

◆ Avoid unnecessary questions.

◆ Avoid awkward constructions and repetitions.

You now have before you a polished report. Prepare a crisp version of the final copy, with photocopies. If you wrote at a word processor, be sure to make a backup of your file for future reference and revision. You may want to experiment with different printer fonts and page layout to make your report attractive.

Take a moment to consider how your short report can be presented most effectively. Instead of sending the report to your manager by office mail, for example, you may decide to deliver the work in person. For longer reports, consider the positive impression made by a tasteful binding (available at print and photocopy shops).

SAMPLE SHORT REPORT

Policies on Maternity Leave at EEW, Inc.

Submitted to
The Executive Board

by

Margery Vickers
Sheldon Ramirez
Codirectors, Personnel Department

January 6, 20___

Table of Contents

I. Executive Summary

From 1995 to 2000, EEW, Inc., granted no maternity leaves for pregnant workers. As a result, more than 50 pregnant workers per year quit their jobs. Less than 10 percent returned after delivery. Late in 2000 the company began granting selective maternity leaves, without pay, based on an employee's record of accomplishment. Because few employees applied for such payless leaves and fewer received them, resignations due to pregnancy still totaled 40 to 45 workers per year in the time period 2000–2001. Since that time, company policy has been liberalized to permit pregnant workers to take maternity leave, still without pay, but with no loss of position in seniority if they return to work within six months. While this policy has helped to stem the steady flow of resignations due to pregnancy, the company should consider a policy of maternity leave with half pay as an effective way to retain trained employees and, in the long term, to save money.

iii

II. Overview

Motivated by Federal and State Legislation, union demands, and its own interests, EEW has assigned the personnel department the task of reporting on past, present, and future company policies regarding maternity leave among company workers. This report details past practices, summarizes present policies, and evaluates the factors that will guide future policy.

The report concludes that EEW should provide up to four months maternity leave, with half pay. These measures, while not yet common among our competitors, are justified in the report on the basis of employee retention and long-term savings to the company.

III. Past Policies on Maternity Leave at EEW

At the time of the company's founding in 1995, it had no written policy for pregnancy or maternity leave. Workers routinely quit their jobs when they discovered their pregnancy or were dismissed when the pregnancy became obvious to their supervisors. Company personnel files show that a few workers requested leaves of absence without pay for the period of their pregnancy and the months after. Without exception, these requests were turned down by the company. In the words of an infamous internal memo from the now-deceased former president of the company: "Absolutely no. If she has one child, she'll probably have more. There is no end to that kind of thing."[1]

Under pressure from union negotiators and women's groups, the company in 1996 began to grant leaves without pay to workers who had demonstrated a record of achievement and promise. While no statistics can be gathered to make the point in a concrete way, many pregnant workers still were dismissed in the late 1990s

1

on the grounds that their records weren't "promising enough." Despite repeated efforts by the company's personnel director during those years, management resisted all efforts to set forth clear work standards by which "enough" could be measured. Pregnant employees well into 2001, therefore, found themselves dependent upon the whim of a supervisor for a leave of absence, of course without pay.

In 2002, a watershed event changed the company's policies overnight. Interestingly, this event came not from legislation or external pressure. A talented vice president of the company proudly announced her pregnancy to a somewhat shocked board meeting on Jan. 2, 2002. She went on to speak of her commitment to the company and her earnest desire to take up her duties again as soon as possible after giving birth.

A discussion ensued, pitting the traditionalists in the company against those interested in finding new and more flexible policies. Traditionalists argued that profits, not parenthood, were the sole concern of the company. Pregnant employees, they said, could not be retained, nor could their positions be held open for them. More liberal minds argued that companies had far-reaching obligations to their employees and could not simply turn them out for choosing to bear children.

The pregnant vice president brought both groups up short in a brief statement still recorded in the minutes of that meeting: "Let me put it this way, gentlemen. I led the successful company effort to attract over $4 million in contracts and grants last year. I have an offer to do that kind of work for your main competitor during my pregnancy and after. I spoke of my commitment to this company. Now you must decide if I'm worth your commitment. In the long term,

2

will I make you enough money to compensate for my pregnancy leave?"[2] At that point she smiled and left the meeting.

As a result of that meeting, she was offered a leave of absence without pay for the last three months of her pregnancy and the first three months of motherhood. (Incidentally, she left the company to accept an identical offer <u>with</u> pay from the competitor.) Leaves without pay were available from that time on to other pregnant workers. Relatively few workers took such leaves, however, because they could not afford to live for that period without an income. They opted instead for unemployment compensation or other work that allowed them to earn right up to the date of delivery.

IV. Present Policies

Since January 2002, the personnel department sponsored a successful drive in the company to allow pregnant workers to stay at their occupations with the company as long as their personal physician would allow. Barring company-wide layoffs, these workers could return to their jobs within six months after giving birth, without loss of seniority or pay level.[3]

That policy continues to the present. No salary is paid during leaves of absence due to pregnancy. Benefits may be paid, depending upon the benefit package selected by the employee.

At present, the workforce of EEW totals 1,152 workers, of which 802 are women. While the personnel department does not claim to know of every pregnancy among the workers, we estimate that each year fifty to sixty workers become pregnant with the intention of bearing a child. Of this number, no more than 10 percent apply for a leave without pay for the period of pregnancy and delivery.[4]

3

V. Evaluation

Those pregnant workers who do not request a leave of absence simply quit. Few return to the company in later months or years. As illustrated in Figure 1, these resignations result in a substantial loss to the company each year. Note in the chart that an employee usually requires at least five months to reach the production level of our average experienced employee:

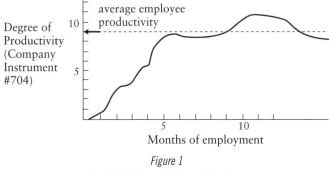

Figure 1
Productivity During First Year of Employment

During this period of learning, the company is paying out an average salary of $2,000 per month, only a percentage of which is earned by employee production during the learning process. Thus, the company invests an average $5,000 in the training of each employee, as demonstrated in the following table.

Month	Salary	Production %	Training Cost
1	$2,000	10%	$1,800
2	$2,000	30%	$1,400
3	$2,000	50%	$1,000
4	$2,000	70%	$ 600
5	$2,000	90%	$ 200
		Total	$5,000

4

In addition to this $5,000 spent in training, the Personnel Department spends on average $1,240 in advertising, interviewing, and processing costs for each new employee hired.[5]

Therefore, if 50 workers quit per year due to pregnancy, the company cost in wasted training, advertising, interviewing, and processing is $312,000 [50 × ($5,000 + $1,240)].

For prudent policy decisions on pregnancy, that substantial sum must be weighed against the cost of simply providing half pay for pregnant workers during the last month of pregnancy and the first three months of motherhood. Assuming that all 50 workers accepted such an arrangement, the company would pay 50 × 1,000 (half pay) × 4 months = $200,000.

The resultant saving to the company under such a plan would be $112,000. More difficult to measure but equally important are such advantages to the company as improved employee morale, enhanced company image for job seekers, and fewer trainees in the workforce.

VI. Conclusion

Over the nine years of the company's existence, policies on pregnancy leave have been steadily liberalized in favor of the worker. Based on the training and replacement costs set forth in this report, the trend toward partial salary during pregnancy leave is in the financial interest of the company. EEW will spend one-third less to retain pregnant employees through half pay leaves than to lose them and pay for advertising, interviewing, processing, and training for replacements.

5

Appendix: Five Case Studies

All aspects of the following five cases are factually true. Names have been changed to protect privacy.

1998—Ruth

After two years with the company as an accountant, Ruth asked her supervisor for leave without pay during her pregnancy and first few months of motherhood. The request was routinely denied. Ruth resigned her position at EEW, had her baby, then found employment with EEW's main competitor, Technoelectric Designs. Today Ruth heads the accounting division at that company. Recently she was honored by the National Accounting Association for innovative and money-saving approaches to economic forecasting at Technoelectric.

1999—Jan

Fearing that she would be fired, Jan hid her pregnancy as best she could into the sixth month. Her supervisor recommended her dismissal at that time in spite of Jan's excellent work record at EEW. Jan's husband, a senior engineer at EEW, expressed outrage at the handling of the situation. Both found employment elsewhere.

2000—Francine

An assembly-line worker, Francine requested a leave of absence without pay. Her request was turned down because her work record, in the words of the rejection memo, "did not merit such concessions by the company." Acting through her union, Francine took the matter before the National Labor Relations Board and won a judgment against the company. After receiving back pay and a settlement, Francine voluntarily found employment at Micro-Circuitry, Inc. She now supervises an assembly unit there.

6

2001—Barbara

Barbara applied for and received maternity leave without pay. She left EEW in the fifth month of her pregnancy. Faced with rising financial obligations, however, she found temporary work at Technoelectric Designs during the latter months of her pregnancy. A few weeks after delivery, she returned to the workforce, but not at EEW. She manages the sales support at Technoelectric Designs today.

2002—Cathy

Cathy in early 2002 came to the personnel department for counseling. She and her husband planned to start a family, she said, but could do so only if she could be assured of returning to her job a few weeks after delivery. The personnel officer explained that she could return to her job up to six months after delivery. Cathy kept her job at EEW, returning two months after her baby was born. She resigned a few months later, explaining in her exit interview that she and her husband were making plans for another child. She wanted to find employment with a company that offered some kind of financial support during pregnancy leave.

Endnotes

1. <u>Annual Personal Summary, 1994</u>, Vol. IV, p. 68.
2. <u>Corporate Minutes</u>, Oct. 2002, p. 137.
3. For a full description of this policy, see <u>Personnel Policies and Procedures</u>, 2002, pp. 387–98.
4. This figure is based upon leave applications formally filed with the Personnel Department during the 2002 fiscal year.
5. For a detailed explanation of this estimated average, see <u>Internal Economic Report No. 7</u>, Jan. 2002, p. 204.

7

SUMMARY KEYS FOR WRITING A GREAT SHORT REPORT

1. Remember that your short report will probably be used as the basis for important decision-making. In your report, provide the arguments and evidence needed for such decisions.

2. Generating ideas for short reports is a vital first step toward your goal of a complete, concise document. Gathering more ideas than you can use is preferable to stretching a few ideas beyond their worth.

3. The core structure of a short report lies in its argument, supported by appropriate evidence. That argument should be evident in the headings and subheadings used in the short report.

Chapter 9

◆

Writing Winning Proposals and Short Business Plans:

Designing Persuasive Arguments

◆

The parts of a proposal find their place according to one criterion: the role they play in the overall purpose of the document.

This chapter shows how to take great business ideas—the kind that occur to you in the middle of the night, perhaps, or over dinner conversation—and capture them for yourself and others in words that communicate your vision and motivate action. Unfortunately, too many great ideas evaporate simply because someone did not have the skill or energy to commit them to words in the form of a proposal or business plan.

Contracts and venture capital funding do not simply arrive on a company's doorstep. They are earned through written words, most often in the form of proposals and business plans.

PROPOSALS

Although proposals differ according to use and length, most are made up of an overview, a problem analysis, proposal specifics and benefits, a budget or other resource breakdown, and an action-oriented conclusion. These five parts are treated in detail later in this chapter.

The parts of a proposal find their place according to one criterion: the role they play in the overall purpose of the document. The central purpose of a business proposal, for example, is to persuade readers to act. All parts of the proposal, therefore, must be arranged to serve this purpose. In writing winning proposals, bear in mind three powerful forces that help to persuade your readers:

◆ logical order of ideas

◆ psychological order of ideas

◆ solid support for ideas

LOGICAL ORDER

The chain of logic in a proposal can be viewed like a row of dominoes. Each acts upon the next in an onward movement toward the conclusion of the proposal. Only a missing link—a logical flaw— can halt the onward force of logical order in the proposal.

Consider, for example, the sequence of logical steps at the heart of a proposal to install brighter streetlights in a residential neighborhood:

Point 1: Residents care most of all about safety and property values.
Point 2: Brighter streetlights discourage crime, thereby making the neighborhood more safe.
Point 3: Brighter streetlights increase property values, because safer areas have higher property values.
Point 4: Residents can be expected to support the proposal, because it gives them what they want—safety and higher property values.

This logical design is not complex, but it serves to illustrate the domino effect of logical argumentation. One point leads to the next, which in turn leads to a directly related point. Taken together, the points lead to a logical conclusion.

LOGICAL FLAWS

In developing a logical design for your proposals, be on guard against ten common logical flaws in argumentation:

1. *Circular Reasoning.* What was intended as an explanation is in fact a mere restatement.

> *All employees are encouraged to participate in after-hours company recreation programs because such programs are especially for the use of employees after the workday has ended.*

2. *Hasty Generalization.* The conclusion reached is based on too little evidence.

> *Democrats can't win the election because of their stand on the electoral college.*

3. *Non Sequitur.* A conclusion is reached that does not follow from the evidence presented.

> *Johnson owns two homes, a boat, and a sports car. Therefore I trust his investment advice.*

4. *Bias.* Personal opinion becomes the standard for evaluating objective argument.

> *Ms. Wilmington has every right to apply for the new position, but she won't get it. I just don't think a woman belongs in this job.*

5. *Either/Or Thinking.* Two alternatives are presented as the only alternatives when others should also be considered.

> *Either he apologizes or I quit.*

6. *False Cause.* An earlier occurrence is incorrectly presented as the cause of a later event.

> *We switched to leased cars instead of company-owned cars last year. No wonder we now have so many repair bills.*

7. *Straw Man.* A false target is set up for the main thrust of an argument. Knocking over the straw man creates the illusion that the argument has succeeded.

> *This company's problems can be blamed on poor benefits. How can anyone expect workers to concentrate on their jobs when they have doubts about their medical and dental coverage?*

8. *Faulty Syllogism.* A flawed pattern of logic leads to an unjustifiable conclusion.

> *All managers have moustaches. I have a moustache. Therefore I am a manager.*

9. *Stacking the Argument.* Evidence is presented on one side of an issue while ignoring evidence on the other side.

> *Undersea mining operations are expensive and time-consuming. We should not consider undersea mining in deciding how and where to mine for gold.*

10. *False Elimination.* From an array of possible alternatives, one by one is eliminated until only one alternative remains. The illusion is thereby created that the final alternative is the best.

> *In reviewing cities for our company move, we've seen why Toledo, Miami, Dallas, Chicago, and Milwaukee won't meet our needs. That leaves Phoenix as the logical choice for our new company headquarters.*

PSYCHOLOGICAL ORDER

Skilled writers of proposals try to influence the feelings of their readers as well as their thoughts. They want readers to agree with the ideas of the document. One technique used by such writers is the careful placement and timing of good news and bad news in proposals.

The Placement of Bad News

Bad news can be defined as a message that threatens our welfare, stability, or reputation. A manager may hear the bad news that his or her division is being reduced in size and importance. A company may hear the bad news that it faces a major lawsuit.

Proposal writers don't shy away from bad news. Instead, they recognize that bad news sets the stage—the necessary precondition—for good news. Bad news forms the question, in a sense, that the good news (the proposed idea) attempts to answer. Consider, for example a major proposal for road improvements on a mountain pass highway. The bad news is that several accidents have occurred because of poor road conditions, particularly during bad weather. The proposal writer explains the causes of these accidents in detail, all in preparation for the proposed solution of repaving, posting better signs, and setting strict speed limits.

The Placement of Good News

Good news may be welcomed by every reader, but that does not mean it will be believed by every reader. Good news must be presented in a way as to seem not only possible but probable. This entails careful analysis of what the reader may resist in the good news being presented.

In the case of a proposal for land development, for example, the proposal writer might point to three items of potential good news for those interested in investing in the venture:

◆ Housing prices have never been higher.

◆ The exclusive area in question has only a few remaining tracts for development.

◆ The architect has worked up creative initial renderings of the kinds of homes that can be built.

Each of these items of good news falls flat, however, if the proposal writer does not take into account the resistance that may be felt by readers. If housing prices are higher than ever before, will there be a market for the finished homes? If the exclusive area has only a few undeveloped lots, have they remained undeveloped for a reason, such as permit problems, drainage, and so on? Finally, will the architect's creative plans prove economically feasible?

Delivering good news, then, requires timing and sensitivity to related issues. Bright, desirable ideas must face and overcome whatever obstacles are presented in the reader's mind before they can become influential ideas.

SOLID EVIDENCE

Readers are swayed to accept ideas by the skilled use of evidence in the form of examples, illustrations, statistics, and details. Such evidence can be general or specific in nature.

General evidence is made up of a great number of specific examples gathered together (or generalized). "The air in metropolitan areas is 16 percent cleaner this year because of federal pollution legislation," is an example of general evidence.

By contrast, specific evidence treats precise details of a single case: "Air quality measurements during the month of July in Los Angeles show a 16 percent improvement in overall air quality." Specific evidence, especially when supported by reputable and knowledgeable sources, helps to convince the reader that the proposal writer's major ideas are sound.

Successful proposal writers mix both general and specific evidence to create a case for their ideas. Too much general evidence makes a proposal sound vague and unfocused. Too much specific evidence can make a proposal sound narrow, local, and parochial in its concerns. When these are balanced, however, general and specific evidence can earn the reader's acceptance of ideas within a proposal.

PROPOSAL WRITING STRATEGIES

Proposals are a common means by which businesses and individuals attract contracts, obtain research money, change in-house procedures, fund new facilities, or argue for product or policy revisions. Use this step-by-step guide to construct practical, successful proposals.

STEP ONE:
Determine requirements for your proposal

Specific guidelines may already exist for developing your proposal. For example, many government agencies have strict requirements for the way topics are described, the order in which they are treated, the length of the proposal, and so forth. Some of these requirements may strike you as unnecessary and even inane. However, you should never purposely break the assigned guidelines issued by a granting agency or client without written permission to do so.

STEP TWO:
Determine who will evaluate your proposal

Find out whether your work will be read by content specialists or by a more general audience. Choose language designed to communicate clearly to your readers.

Jot down ideas, examples, and details that fit this audience; you will use these materials in the outlining and drafting stages.

STEP THREE:
Create an outline for your proposal

By developing an outline of your major points, you can see at a glance the flow and coherence of your argument and evidence. The following major categories appear in most proposal outlines:

I. Overview
Provide the background information your reader will need to grasp the significance of your proposed idea and to acquaint the reader with the nature and scope of your argument. Answer such questions as, Why is the proposal needed? Who will benefit? Why should the proposal be accepted? When must readers act upon the proposal? What are your objectives in the proposal? How does your approach differ from other approaches?

II. Problem Analysis
If you want your proposed idea to strike the reader as necessary and timely—an action item—set the stage by analyzing the problem with care. What caused the problem? Who suffers from its effects? What measures have failed in an effort to deal with it? What is the current scale of the problem? What will be its future scale? These questions suggest the kind of analysis to do in this section of the proposal. Use both general and specific evidence to make your case.

III. Proposal Specifics

Describe in detail your proposed plan of attack. Are your methods proven? If so, how and by whom? What personnel will be involved? What is their training? What time schedule have you established for completing work? What are major checkpoints in that schedule?

Also discuss how you plan to evaluate your proposed enterprise. What significant indications of progress will you look for? When? How will you measure success?

Conclude this section with a summary estimation—a convincing statement of the likelihood that your plans will produce the results desired. Often, proposal writers describe their ultimate goals as a series of achievement plateaus, any one of which justifies the work proposed. In this way, writers allow funding agencies to feel that even if the highest predictions of the proposal bear no fruit, important results can nonetheless be accomplished at plateaus along the way.

The summary estimation is the writer's last chance to persuade readers before introducing a key proposal element: a clear statement of money required, usually with a description of its intended uses.

IV. The Budget

Outline the costs of your proposed work, including the following items if applicable:

◆ equipment acquisition

◆ facility rental

◆ salary and wages

◆ supplies

◆ travel expenses

◆ research expenses

◆ contingency funds

Proposal writers sometimes make the mistake of padding their budgets, in expectation of receiving only a portion of what they request. They apply the "two for one" rule: Determine what is really needed, ask for twice as much, and hope to end up with what was needed in the first place. That game is played with less and less success these days. Padded budgets usually don't slip by shrewd evaluators who review proposals in business, science, and government.

V. Conclusion

A proposal should not begin or end with a dollar sign. Conclude your proposal by expressing your willingness to help your readers. Offer to answer questions and to provide further information, to meet with or speak by phone to evaluators, referees, or others, and even to consider reshaping the proposal as necessary to meet the needs of the client or agency.

STEP FOUR:
Revise and polish your proposal to make it attractive

Because proposals are often judged competitively, they must win attention and respect by how they look as well as by what they say. Here are five ways to give your proposals a crisp, professional appearance:

◆ Use your word processor's most attractive, proportionately spaced fonts.

◆ Print on heavy-bond white paper.

◆ Use consistent margins on all sides of the page.

◆ Decide whether your proposal will have a more powerful effect in bound form, with a vinyl or heavy paper cover (usually in a conservative color). Most photocopy and fast-print shops can bind your work inexpensively.

◆ Make sure that photocopied versions of your proposal are comparable to the original in clarity. Check to make sure that all copied pages appear in the right order.

CHECKLIST FOR EFFECTIVE REVISION

Successful revision of a document draft is much like a successful physical checkup. Like a skilled doctor, the writer first looks at the big picture:

◆ Does the document meet the needs of the audience?

◆ Does the document have a clear, stated purpose?

◆ Is the tone and style of the document appropriate for the audience and circumstances?

Next the writer examines the parts:

◆ Does the introduction announce the subject and the approach the writer will take?

◆ Are paragraphs well-formed, with topic sentences supported by argument, evidence, examples, details, and/or statistics?

◆ Are paragraphs linked by clear transitions? Are sentences within paragraphs linked by clear transitions?

◆ Do internal summaries appear, where needed, to recap major points?

◆ In longer documents, are headings provided to guide the reader's understanding?

Finally, the writer reviews a number of specific matters having to do with style and correctness:

◆ Does the frequent use of the active voice make for lively, energetic reading?

◆ Are sentence types varied for pleasing prose rhythms?

◆ Are key words and ideas emphasized by proper placement within sentences and paragraphs?

◆ Has specific, concrete language been substituted for unnecessarily abstract language?

◆ Has wordiness been eliminated?

◆ Has parallelism been used in lists and series?

◆ Have pronouns been used with care, especially the vague *this* and *that*?

◆ Have paragraph length and sentence length been controlled for emphasis and readability?

◆ Have trite and slang expressions been eliminated?

◆ Have unnecessary questions been rephrased as clear statements?

◆ Have awkward constructions and repetitions been rephrased?

◆

SAMPLE PROPOSAL

A Shuttle Service for State University

proposed to
The Board of Trustees
State University

Submitted by

Student Body Association

May 16, 20___

EXECUTIVE SUMMARY

The Student Body Association urges the Board of Trustees to approve the expenditure of $36,000 for a one-semester pilot test of a student/faculty shuttle bus at State University. The shuttle would alleviate parking problems, increase safety, reduce air pollution, and save money both for the university and for its members. The Student Body Association offers its human and financial resources in support of the pilot project.

OVERVIEW

Each year university administrators, faculty, staff, and students share a common complaint: too little parking on campus. Because most student living quarters and faculty homes do not lie within comfortable walking distance, particularly during the winter, most members of the university community drive a car to campus. A Student Body Association survey during fall semester, 20__, showed 2,945 automobiles being driven to campus each weekday. Sixty-eight percent of those automobiles traveled less than two miles to campus from home. The great majority (82 percent) contained only one person. Arriving on campus, these drivers found limited and expensive ($138 per semester) parking.

The Student Body Association proposes a shuttle bus service from student and faculty living areas within a two-mile radius of the campus.

ASPECTS OF THE PARKING PROBLEM
AT STATE UNIVERSITY

Bounded as it is by residential properties, State University has little chance to expand auxiliary parking areas in the coming years. Nor can a significant portion of campus land be converted to parking because of building plans already approved in the university's master plan.

Therefore, we must consider the university's 2,475 student/faculty/staff parking places relatively fixed for the coming year.

Too Many Cars for Too Few Spaces

These 2,475 spaces cannot accommodate the estimated 3,000 cars per day driven to campus, even though 96 percent of this number have purchased on-campus parking permits. The overflow of approximately 350 cars per day (allowing for half-day parking use of spaces) must currently find parking in residential neighborhoods. This necessity has led to sixteen written complaints by university neighbors to City Hall in the past six months. Clearly, the neighborhoods surrounding State University do not wish to become auxiliary parking lots for students, faculty, and staff.

Walking Is Impractical for Most Students

At recent public hearings on the parking problem, university administrators have cited the Student Body Association survey showing that 68 percent of university commuters drive less than two miles to campus. Could not a substantial portion of those commuters, administrators asked, simply walk to school?

On April 7, 20__, the Student Body Association completed a poll of 500 such university members, selected randomly. Only 9 percent indicated a willingness to walk to campus and, of that number, 76 percent said they would walk only occasionally. Reasons cited by 91 percent who said they would not consider walking include

- difficulty in transporting books and school materials.
- discomfort in bad weather.
- use of an on-campus car for storing books, calculators, gym clothing, and so forth.
- time constraints (leaving campus for a job, for example).

The parking problem, we can safely conclude, will not be resolved by a sudden willingness of State University students, faculty, and staff to walk to campus.

A PROPOSAL TO RELIEVE THE PARKING PROBLEM

The Student Body Association urges the Board of Trustees, at their next regular meeting, to approve the expenditure of $36,000 for a one-semester pilot test of a shuttle service. As detailed below, the shuttle bus would serve students, faculty, and staff within a two-mile radius of the campus.

Transportation consultants donating their services to the Student Body Association estimate that such a shuttle service, operating from 7 a.m. to 7 p.m. weekdays, could provide transportation for approximately 400 students per day. That number exceeds the overflow now using neighborhoods around the university for parking.

A student, faculty, and staff survey completed April 30, 20___, by the Student Body Association showed that 86 percent of a random sample of 500 participants indicated a strong willingness to use shuttle transportation to the university if the cost per ride were 50 cents or less.

We project with some confidence, therefore, that a shuttle pilot program would be accepted by members of the university and would relieve the current parking problem. If the pilot program proves successful, the concept can be replicated for several shuttle buses, each earning its own way from rider revenues.

BUDGETARY CONSIDERATIONS

An expenditure of $36,000 will allow the Student Body Association to take the following steps:

1. Rent a state-approved 35 passenger shuttle bus
   for six months $6,000
2. Pay two drivers' wages and benefits for six months.......$24,000
3. Pay for garage expenses, upkeep, and contingencies...... $6,000
                          Total Expenditure $36,000

We project that at a conservative rate of 400 paying rides per weekday at 50 cents per ride, the bus will produce gross revenues of $1,000 per week, netting approximately $400 after gas and oil expenses. It is the intention of the Student Body Association to apply this net profit to the repayment of the $36,000 pilot fund. Over the course of six months (26 weeks), this repayment can amount to as much as $10,400 (26 weeks × $400 net profit per week). If the shuttle bus becomes more popular than we have estimated, the repayment figure will be even higher.

The Student Body Association agrees to repay the $36,000 expenditure in full from profits arising out of a shuttle service growing out of a pilot program before any profits are distributed to the Association itself.

CONCLUSION

Because it offers the best alternative for alleviating the severe parking problem faced by members of the university, the Shuttle Pilot Program deserves the serious consideration of the Board of Trustees.

The Officers of the Student Body Association will be happy to elaborate upon aspects of this proposal and to answer questions of the Board. We look forward to working with you in serving the needs of our mutual constituency.

◆

THE SHORT BUSINESS PLAN

Proposals intended to create or restructure business opportunities are called business plans. These documents may be as short as a few pages (communicating a new business concept, for example) or as long as a thick book (including financial information, product or service descriptions, corporate officers' biographical sketches, and more). Whether long or short, all business plans attempt to answer crucial questions for the potential investor or authorizing executive, such as:

◆ What is the basic idea of your plan?

◆ What products or services will your business produce or provide?

◆ How will you market and sell your wares or services?

◆ How will you organize and manage your business?

◆ How will finances be handled?

◆ What do you want from your reader?

The Basic Business Idea

In an executive summary, provide the following information as concisely as possible:

◆ What kind of business activity you intend to pursue

◆ Why your business appears financially attractive

◆ Who will manage and staff your organization

◆ Where you will base your business

◆ How much money your business will require for start-up and other expenses

◆ What an investor or authorizing company can expect to gain for its support

The Business Concept

Begin the body of the business plan itself by explaining and justifying the business concept. Describe the parts or processes involved in the concept.

Relate the concept to all necessary background information about how the concept began. Be sure to discuss how your product or service compares to your competitors' and show why yours will be more profitable.

Products and Services

In this section, describe the products or services generated by your business concept. Pictures and other graphics may be useful here. Sell your product or service in this portion of the business plan.

Marketing and Sales

Give a detailed account of your marketing strategies for the business. Tell who will be likely to buy your products or services and why. Back up your assertions with marketing data, demographic information, and other evidence.

Business Organization

Describe what kind of organization you will establish to produce your products or services. Define how the company will be managed and run. Emphasize the qualifications of your managers and officers.

Company Finances

Specify how much money will be required, and at what stages, for start-up costs and contingencies. Provide a rationale for how money will be spent. Describe how profits and potential losses will be treated with regard to investors. Be as specific and realistic as possible, but be sure to highlight the positive aspects of your financial analysis.

Conclusion and Action Steps

In this section, give specifics of the business offering itself, including how much money you are seeking from investors, and in what installments. Describe the investors' degree of liability for company operations and the terms of their financial participation in company profits.

In a business world in which more than 80 percent of new businesses have gone broke by their fifth anniversary, a business plan must forcefully persuade potential investors to take a risk. As recently reported in *The Wall Street Journal*, one venture capital firm received 1,200 business plans over a period of six months for funding consideration. Of that number, the firm selected only 45 for serious consideration. Of that number, only 14 were eventually funded—a little more than 1 in 100. In that kind of competitive environment, only the best-prepared business plans survive.

SAMPLE BUSINESS PLAN

TeleCycle

A Business Plan

prepared for

Armstrong Funding Associates
Salt Lake City, Utah

by

Richard R. Foster
Michelle Ames

January 15, 20__

(Proprietary)

Executive Summary

Americans will purchase 5,500,000 new telephones in 20__ for business and residential use. In the process, they will dispose of approximately 3,000,000 telephones in good working order. This trend can be expected to continue throughout this decade as new advances in telephone technology and design cause increasing numbers of Americans to replace their present telephones.

TeleCycle, as proposed in this business plan, represents a highly profitable channel for recycling these telephones to foreign markets and both domestic and international industrial uses. The TeleCycle plan will persuade Americans by the millions to trade, not trash, their present telephones.

The method of operation is straightforward. TeleCycle representatives will contract with major telephone suppliers to advertise $5 off the purchase price of a new telephone with a trade-in of an older phone in any condition. TeleCycle will reimburse these suppliers on a 50 percent basis—that is, $2.50 for every telephone delivered to TeleCycle.

TeleCycle will, in turn, refurbish and repair these telephones before selling them, in lots of 100, to foreign markets. Unrepairable telephones will be disassembled for usable materials to be sold for domestic and international industrial use. Market research has defined a large and untapped foreign market for working telephones in the $6 to $8 range per unit.

Based on this market potential, TeleCycle will begin proposed operations with an initial capitalization of $400,000, 25 percent of which is already on deposit as the contribution of the principals to the business. The business seeks twelve investment units of $25,000 each to accrue the remaining $300,000. Each unit will earn 4 percent of the company's net profit per year, in perpetuity, for a total investor interest in the company of 48 percent. The principals will retain a 52 percent share of profits.

I. The Business Concept

Recycling has proven to be one of the most popular and profitable industries of the new century, as Americans become more sensitized and motivated by environmental concerns. Glass recycling, for example, has grown to a $2 billion business, with average profits per major firm in the 12–14 percent range. Aluminum recycling has shown a $234 million total profit for six companies in fiscal 20__.

The TeleCycle concept involves a similar appeal to the American people to recycle what they are no longer using—their old telephones. These units are omnipresent on the storage shelves of American homes and businesses. By the *Consumer Reports'* estimate of 20__, Americans are now storing over 11 million telephones. The vast majority of these will find their way eventually to the trash.

At the same time, Americans are buying new telephones in record numbers. *Consumer Reports* estimates that 5.5 million telephones will be sold by major distributors in 20__. In most cases, those customers could—and generally would like to—carry in their old telephones for a $5 credit toward their purchase.

Working closely with major distributors acting as collection centers for these telephones, TeleCycle will then repair or disassemble the units for resale. We project primary markets for repaired telephones to be Central America, South America, Africa, China, and Russia.

II. TeleCycle Products and Service

TeleCycle will contract with major new telephone distributors to pay a flat $2.50 rate per traded unit and to pick up these units from the distributors' central collection sites.

Based on test market studies, we estimate that 70 percent of the traded telephones will be in good working order and will require only cleansing before being packed for shipment and sale. Of the remaining 30 percent, we estimate that half will be easily repairable (less than $2 in parts and 10 minutes in technician time) and the other half valuable only for parts and raw materials.

All evaluation, sorting, repair, and packing of telephones will take place at TeleCycle's proposed dockside warehouse in San Francisco.

III. The Business Process

At least eleven foreign countries maintain open orders, through governmental and private sources, for as many telephones as they can purchase in the $6 to $8 range. Depending on international availability, used telephone prices in the period 20__ to 20__ have ranged from a low of $4.50 to a high of $14. For the next five years, we project an average wholesale price per unit to be $8 and have based our financial structure on that conservative projection.

TeleCycle will make contact with major buyers of telephone equipment in selected foreign countries through their commercial officers, attached to embassies in Washington, D.C. Preliminary contacts with ten such officers have provided us with several bona fide purchase offers for used telephones in large lots. We also have had strong interest in the purchase of telephone parts and recyclable materials from domestic and international industries.

IV. The Marketing Plan

TeleCycle will market its services in four distinct ways:

1. Decision-makers at a wide range of new telephone distribution sources will be initially contacted by a professionally prepared prospectus and proposal, delivered by express mail.

2. Follow-up calls will be made by the TeleCycle principals and their representatives to bring these distributors aboard as contracted partners.

3. Advance advertising through foreign trade journals, magazines, and other media will alert foreign buyers to this new, substantial source for used telephones. The wave of their interest, in turn, will be used as evidence to further convince American distributors to join the program.

4. As soon as a limited number of distributors have contracted with TeleCycle, the company will begin a nationwide publicity campaign, primarily through newspaper and radio advertisements, to alert Americans to recycle their telephones. Our initial contacts with the Environmental Protection Agency and the American Advertising Council have given us strong reason to believe that many of these advertisements may be carried as low-cost public service ads.

Once a stable network of distributors is in place, TeleCycle will employ a field staff of commissioned salespeople in carefully selected countries and regions to seek out quantity buyers of used telephone equipment.

V. Financial Information

Capital Outlay

Of the first-year $400,000 capitalization, approximately equal fourths will be assigned for the following uses:

$100,000   Staff salaries for two technicians and two secretaries. (The principals will not draw salary during the first year of operations.)

$100,000   Warehouse and office leasing and furnishing, two transport vans, overhead.

$100,000   Printing, advertising.

$100,000   Operations.

Projected Income

Based on a profit percentage of 60 percent (after repair and shipping expenses) for each used telephone unit sold, TeleCycle projects the following volume and revenues for the next three years:

Year	Units Sold	Gross Income	Net Profit
Start-up	90,000	$ 720,000	$ 432,000
2	200,000	$1,600,000	$ 930,000
3	340,000	$2,720,000	$1,632,000

Based on these projections, an investor holding a 4 percent share of net profit could expect, for the $25,000 investment, a first-year payout of $17,280, a second-year payout of $37,200 and a third-year payout of $65,280, with successive years following a similar upward curve.

VI. Management

TeleCycle will be directed by two MBAs with substantial experience in the telephone industry.

[Brief bios appear here for Richard Foster and Michelle Ames.]

VII. Specifics of the Business Offering

For investors interested in one or more units (at $25,000 per unit) of this venture, we will be pleased to provide copies of a contractual limited partnership agreement. Upon investor approval of the document, we request payment in the form of a cashier's check payable to TeleCycle, Inc. Individual investors may each own up to four units. The company seeks to place a total of twelve units with investors.

Thank you for your interest in the TeleCycle business concept and plan. The principals will be pleased to meet with individual investors or their representatives.

◆

SUMMARY KEYS FOR WRITING WINNING PROPOSALS AND SHORT BUSINESS PLANS

1. Readers are persuaded not only by the logical design of a proposal but also by its psychological design, in terms of its placement of good news and bad news.

2. Logical flaws can short-circuit the persuasiveness of proposals and business plans, no matter how well written in other regards.

3. Writers use both general and specific evidence where appropriate to support assertions and argument.

Chapter 10

Changing and Rearranging:

Fast Fixes for the Final Polish

◆

The final look of your document matters as much as all the hard work you've poured into its language and content.

This chapter reminds you that your readers never see the minutes or hours of hard work you have poured into the development of your document. All they see is the finished product on the page. The care you take in editing and revising will account in large part for the success of your communication.

Count on it: the last five minutes you spend on your letter or memo are infinitely more valuable than the first five minutes you spend on it.

Unfortunately, many business writers skip that last five minutes. You know the result. Letters and memos go out filled with errors in fact, logic, spelling, grammar, and punctuation. Just as serious are unrevised errors in tone—those snarling or petty messages that, with a moment's review, would have been (and should have been) reconsidered.

LEARNING TO LIKE REVISION
Like revision? That's a tall order, especially when business writing itself may not be high on your list of cuddly things.

Writers sometimes have the mistaken notion that revision is a form of assassination—killing inch by inch the gorgeous flow of the first draft. They associate revision with a Mr. or Ms. Gradgrind, English instructor, at some time in their education. Picky, picky, picky.

But contrast that negative mindset with the attitudes of other creators toward their works. A painter looks at the final touchups of a painting as perfecting it, not fretting over it. A musician looks forward to checking out the notes for the final score; without such checking, the performance may sound like fingernails on a blackboard. Writers, too, should learn to revise with pleasure.

A STEP-BY-STEP PLAN FOR REVISION

The final check and revision of letters and memos may be more palatable if it happens in five quick steps.

STEP ONE:

Does your main message stand out?

Reread your letter or memo from the point of view of your reader. Can you quickly locate the clear, concise statement of your main message? Or is it found here and there all over the page, half-buried in long paragraphs?

Solutions:

◆ Use short, direct sentences to state your main message.

◆ Put your main message in a short paragraph by itself.

◆ Tell your reader when you reach your main idea: "Here's what I conclude . . .," "I can sum up the situation as follows . . .," "The most important point is . . ."

STEP TWO:
Will your language appeal to your reader?

Think about the words you've used in your letter or memo. How will your reader interpret those words? Will your message sound too bureaucratic? Too academic? Too slangy or chatty?

Solutions:

◆ Trust common, simple words to carry your meaning. Use jargon and intellectual verbiage only when such words communicate better than any others.

◆ Read your message aloud. Wherever your language sounds awkward or obtuse, use your ordinary conversational phrasing of the idea as your best guide.

STEP THREE:
Do your ideas hang together logically and persuasively?

Readers don't like to reassemble your thoughts like a jigsaw puzzle to determine your intended message. Think through the progress of your ideas to make sure they connect in a clear, cogent way.

Solutions:

◆ As you reread your message, mentally paraphrase the gist of your idea in each paragraph. You'll quickly discover whether your ideas march in a straight line.

◆ Review the common pitfalls in letter and memo logic listed earlier. Reread your message with a sharp eye out for their presence.

STEP FOUR:
Is your letter or memo free of surface errors?

How would you feel taking advice from a financial counselor who couldn't add? Going to a physician who misspells the name of the operation you'll undergo? In the same way, your credibility depends in part upon your mastery of all the little things in writing—correct spelling, grammar, usage, punctuation, capitalization, and so forth. The Quick Guide to Grammar and Punctuation at the end of this book covers most of the items that matter most (and are neglected most often by business writers).

Solutions:

◆ Use a spell-checker, but don't depend on it to correct incorrect word forms ("bare" where you intended "bear," "it" where you intended "is").

◆ Read your document aloud to discover omitted words. The eye skips quickly past portions of the sentence that the voice won't ignore.

◆ Scan your letter or memo from back to front to pick up spelling mistakes. Reading forward makes us aware of content more than word forms; reading backward highlights the words themselves.

STEP FIVE:

How does your letter or memo look on the page?

The final look of your document matters as much as all the hard work you've poured into its language and content. Examine your paragraphs: Too many long ones? Too many short ones? Check out your margins: Wide enough for easy reading? Consistent from page to page? Look over your lists and inset passages: Have bullets or numbers been used correctly? Are items within lists worded in parallel structure for easy comparison? Consider your fonts and printing medium: Does the message look dark, crisp, and clear on the page? Have you used italics, boldface, and graphic highlights appropriately? Check for letter or memo elements: Have you included all the components you wished, including reference initials, copy notations, and enclosures?

Solutions:

◆ Ask a coworker or friend to look over your final draft and make suggestions for its improvement. (You don't always have to make such changes, but at least you've had the advantage of another person's point of view.)

◆ Set the document aside for a few hours, then review it at your leisure. In the heat of composition, what looks "good enough" may cry out for revision a few hours later.

◆ Look at memos or letters you've received from the people you're writing to. Do you spot any aspect of their style or format that you should imitate in your messaging? For example, if they have signed their letters "Cordially," should yours end with "Sincerely"? [Probably not.] If they type their name to include "Dr.," should you address your letter to "Ms." or "Mr."? [Again, probably not.]

COMMON MISSPELLED WORDS IN BUSINESS

absence	desperate	incredible
accidentally	dictionary	independence
accommodate	disappearance	interesting
accumulate	disastrous	irresistible
advice	dissatisfied	its, it's
advise	effect	laid
a lot	eligible	lead
allot	embarrass	led
amateur	eminent	lightning
analyze	environment	loneliness
appearance	equipped	loose
arctic	especially	lose
arguing	exaggerate	losing
argument	excellence	marriage
arithmetic	existence	mathematics
athletic	experience	maybe
attendance	familiar	miniature
beginning	February	miracle
beneficial	foreign	mysterious
benefited	forty	necessary
break	fourth	neurotic
Britain	generally	ninety
bureau	government	notable
business	grammar	noticeable
choose	height	occurred
chose	heiress	occurrence
committee	homemade	omitted
conscience	humorous	optimistic
conscious	hygiene	parallel
definitely	immediately	paralyze

pastime	receive	than
performance	receiving	then
personal	referee	their, there, they're
personnel	reference	thorough
physical	referred	through
possession	restaurant	to, too, two
precede	rhythm	tragedy
preferred	sacrilegious	tries
prejudice	schedule	trouble
principal	seize	truly
principle	separate	typically
privilege	sergeant	usually
probably	severely	unbelievable
proceed	sieve	utterance
professor	similar	vaccinate
pronunciation	sophomore	vain
prophecy	stationary	vein
prophesy	stationery	villain
qualm	studying	weather
quarrel	subtle	weird
quiet	successful	wholly
quite	surprise	writing
quizzes	tendency	

WORDS FREQUENTLY CONFUSED

accept: to receive; to give an affirmative answer to.
except: to exclude; to leave out; to omit.

adapt: to accustom oneself to a situation.
adept: proficient or competent in performing a task.
adopt: to take by choice; to put into practice.

affect: to influence (verb).
effect: result or consequence (noun).
effect: to bring about (verb).

all ready: prepared.
already: previously.

all right: completely right.
alright: an incorrect usage of *all right*.

allusion: a reference to something familiar.
illusion: an *image* of an object; a false impression.

among: refers to three or more.
between: refers to two only.

amount: quantity without reference to individual units.
number: a total of counted units.

anyone: any person in general.
any one: a specific person or item.

assay: to evaluate.
essay: to put to a test (verb).
essay: a literary composition (noun).

beside: by the side of.
besides: in addition to.

biannually: two times a year (also, *semiannually*).
biennially: every two years.

borne: past participle of *bear* (to carry, to produce).
born: brought into existence.

can: refers to ability or capability.
may: refers to permission.

capital: a seat of government; money invested; a form of a letter.
capitol: a government building.

complement: that which completes or supplements.
compliment: flattery or praise.

consensus of opinion: redundant; *consensus* means "general opinion."

council: an assembly of persons.
counsel: to advise; advice; an attorney.
consul: a resident representative of a foreign state.
councillor: a member of a council.
counselor: a lawyer or adviser.

credible: believable or acceptable.
creditable: praiseworthy or meritorious.

deference: respect.
difference: unlikeness.

desert: a reward or punishment (noun).
desert: to abandon (verb).
desert: a barren geographical area (noun).
dessert: a course at the end of a meal.

different from;
different than: American usage prefers "different from."

disburse: to make payments; to allot.
disperse: to scatter.

disinterested: neutral; not biased.
uninterested: not concerned with; lacking interest.

disorganized: disordered.
unorganized: not organized or planned.

each other: refers to two.
one another: refers to more than two.

either;
neither: refers to one or the other of two. With *either* use *or*; with *neither* use *nor*.

elicit: to draw forth, usually a comment or response.
illicit: unlawful; illegal.

emigrate: to leave one country to live in another.
immigrate: to come into a country.
migrate: to travel from place to place periodically.

eminent: outstanding; prominent.
imminent: impending, very near, or threatening.
immanent: inherent.

formally: according to convention.
formerly: previously.

imply: to hint at or to allude to in speaking or writing.
infer: to draw a conclusion from what has been said or written.

ingenious: clever, resourceful.
ingenuous: frank, honest, free from guile.

in regards to: incorrect; use *in regard to* or *as regards*.
irregardless: nonstandard for *regardless*.

its: a possessive singular pronoun.
it's: a contraction for *it is*.

later: refers to time; the comparative form of *late*.
latter: refers to the second named of two.

less: smaller quantity than, without reference to units.
fewer: a smaller total of units.

lie, lay, lain: to recline.
lay, laid: to place.

maybe: perhaps (adverb).
may be: indicates possibility (verb).

percent: should be used after a numeral (*20 percent*).
percentage: for quantity or where numerals are not used (a larger *percentage*).

principal: of primary importance (adjective); head of a school; original sum; chief or official.

principle: a fundamental truth.

respectfully: with respect or deference.

respectively: in order named.

sit: to be seated.

set: to put in position.

sometime: at one time or another.

sometimes: occasionally.

stationary: not moving; fixed.

stationery: writing paper or writing materials.

than: used in comparison (conjunction): "Joe is taller than Tom."

then: relating to time (adverb): "First he ran; then he jumped."

their: belonging to them (possessive of *they*).

there: in that place (adverb).

they're: a contraction of the two words *they are*.

to: preposition: "to the store."

too: adverb: "too cold."

two: number: "two apples."

toward;

towards: identical in meaning and used interchangeably; *toward* is preferred.

who's: a contraction of the two words *who is*.

whose: possessive of *who*.

your: a pronoun.

you're: a contraction of the two words *you are*.

CONVERTING REDUNDANT PHRASES TO CONCISE LANGUAGE

Redundant	Concise
absolutely complete	complete
actual experience	experience
adequate enough	adequate
advance planning	planning
any and all	all
ask the question	ask
basic fundamentals	fundamentals
brief in duration	brief
check up on	check
combine together	combine
completely destroy	destroy
continue on	continue
desirable benefits	benefits
disappear from sight	disappear
each and every	each
end result	result
few in number	few
final conclusion	conclusion
joint cooperation	cooperation
large in size	large
mix together	mix
new innovation	innovation
period of time	period
repeat again	repeat
seems apparent	seems
small-sized	small
surround on all sides	surround
true fact, actual fact	fact
ways and means	means

SUMMARY KEYS FOR CHANGING AND REARRANGING

1. Above all, make sure that your main message stands out in your document.

2. Use language that appeals to your reader. A difficult reading experience decreases the chances that your readers will accept your point of view or agree with your recommendations.

3. Edit with extreme care to eliminate all surface errors (grammar, mechanics, punctuation, usage, and spelling) from your final draft.

4. Arrange your words and paragraphs on the page so that it conveys at first glance its professionalism and readability.

Chapter 11

◆

Difficult Letters, Memos, and E-mail:

Writing for Sensitive Situations

◆

What do you say when you disagree with the boss?

This chapter presents techniques and strategies for writing difficult messages—those awkward, intimidating, or sensitive communications that run the risk of embarrassing you or others, tipping the balance one way or another in high-stakes negotiations, or ruffling feathers up and down the pecking order in your organization.

At his retirement party, one IBM executive recently quipped that he spent 80 percent of his writing time on only 5 percent of his letters and memos. He had in mind these five communications infamous for causing writer's block:

◆ discipline messages

◆ requests for raises or promotion

◆ apologies

◆ cover letters to accompany your resume

◆ objections

In these messages more than others, "tone is all"— how you say it matters at least as much as what you say.

PREPARING TO WRITE DIFFICULT MESSAGES

Begin by talking out your message as if your reader were physically present. If you get stuck, start again from the beginning until you can have your say, start to finish.

Do not set pen to paper or fingers to keys until you have not only a clear grasp of what you want to say but also the tone you want to maintain. One way to capture the tone you want is to jot down particularly appropriate phrases from your earlier "out loud" version of the message.

In the letters and memos that follow, I have tried to use generally appropriate language and tone. Your individual circumstances may require quite different words. I hope, however, that these samples suggest useful approaches to the difficult messages that, as one writer says, "cause drops of blood to pop out on the forehead."

The Discipline Message

There's no trick to writing a discipline message to someone headed out the door of the company. If you choose, you can unload both barrels on the misdoer and not lose a wink of sleep.

But a discipline message to an employee you want to or have to keep? That's a different matter. You have to find disciplinary language that leaves room for good working relations and incentives to improve. In short, you have to slap the hand you're holding.

In the following discipline memo, notice that the language focuses on behaviors (what the employee did) instead of on personal characteristic (what the employee is). This distinction leaves room for improvement. Most of us can change what we do, but not what we are.

In reading these messages, you will recognize that many of the situations they discuss would have been dealt with in a personal meeting as well as in writing.

January 8, 20__

> To: Lester Todd
> Security Specialist I

> From: Martha Owens
> Staff Coordinator

Subject: Personal Goal-setting for Reduced Absenteeism

As we discussed yesterday in my office, Lester, your pattern of absenteeism poses a major problem to your continued employment. In the past three months, you have used five sick days without filing the required medical verification and have, in addition, been absent from work six times for the various personal reasons you explained to your supervisor.

I'm putting this reprimand in writing to you to emphasize the seriousness of your absenteeism.

I will consider the coming quarter a probationary period for you. Your supervisor will report to me on a weekly basis regarding your job attendance and performance. If you have unauthorized absences during this period, you will be dismissed. But with commitment on your part, I hope that we can put this matter behind us.

The company pays for extensive counseling services and other resources for employees. You must be the judge of whether these services can be of use to you in avoiding further absences. Jill Davis, Director of Counseling, will be happy to meet with you to describe the services of her center. You can call her at extension 898 to make an appointment.

On a personal level, Lester, I have seen the good work you're capable of and I want to do whatever I can to help you meet the job expectations of the company.

◆

The Request for a Raise or Promotion

How do you blow your own horn without driving people away? In the following memo, a midlevel manager uses appreciation as the bridge to the more touchy matter of asking for a substantial promotion. Notice that the manager doesn't threaten resignation in an explicit way or make claims about how much the competition will pay her. The memo concludes in such a way that the executive reader has some flexibility to respond. The memo would certainly be less successful if the reader had to make a rigid either/or decision.

September 8, 20___

To: Linda Flower
     Vice President, Personnel

From: Ruth Williams
       Personnel Specialist I

Subject: Your perspective on my career path

I've enjoyed my professional associations and work assignments over the past two years at XyTech. I feel a strong commitment to the company and its future.

I'm writing to ask you to consider me for the present opening in our department for Personnel Analyst. The published advertisement for this position specifies five years of prerequisite personnel experience. Although I haven't worked in the field that long, I'm confident I could perform well in this position for three reasons:

◆ I have just completed my M.A. in Human Resource Management at State University. My studies have given me a thorough knowledge of the latest theories and practical applications in HR and personnel responsibilities.

◆ I worked closely with Mark Atrim, the recently retired Personnel Analyst whose position is being filled. Mark asked me to assist him for a period of six months with the "Hire the Best" program. With his help, I learned a great deal about his job activities during that time.

◆ I have excellent working relations not only with coworkers in my department but with employees throughout the company.

These relationships could prove invaluable to the work of the Personnel Analyst.

I would be happy to meet with you to discuss other aspects of my qualifications and preparation for this position. Thank you for your support over the past two years and for your consideration of my strong interest in the Personnel Analyst position.

Apologies
Whether in a letter to a client or a memo to a work associate, apologies are difficult to put into writing. You must say enough to communicate your sincerity, yet not so much as to seem self-punishing.

Here are the circumstances behind the following apology. An advertising account executive completely forgot about inviting a client to a business lunch. The client found himself waiting alone for an hour at a restaurant far from his office. For the account executive, there was no death in the family or car problem. He just blew it.

The following letter reinforces his earlier phone call of apology. Because the client contacted the account executive's boss to find out what happened, the account executive will probably file a blind copy of this apology letter with his boss to show that he has followed up.

April 19, 20__

John R. Robbins
Advertising Director
Tri-Cities Furniture, Inc.
98 Appletree Highway
Seattle, WA 98233

Dear John:

I'm writing to follow up on our phone conversation this morning. I want to repeat my apology for missing our lunch meeting on Monday. I really can't explain what happened; the meeting was very important to me, but I neglected to note it in my calendar. For some reason, I had in mind that we were meeting on Tuesday. At any rate, I feel terrible about my mistake.

I'd like to reschedule our meeting at your convenience—and this time at Chez Albert. I'll call you tomorrow to see if you're available. I do hope you'll give me this second chance. Believe me, your account executive will get to the restaurant early this time!

Thanks for your understanding.

With best regards,

Paul

Paul Neill
Account Executive

◆

Cover Letter to Accompany Your Resume

What's left to say in a cover letter? Your resume has provided details about your education, experience, career goals, special skills, and references. Should a cover letter try to repeat this information in paragraphs?

No. A cover letter that repeats the resume ends up much too long for the applicant's good. In addition, a redundant cover letter can steal the thunder of the resume.

In recent surveys of Fortune 500 companies, personnel directors say that they give most of their attention to the resume, not the cover letter. In some cases, personnel directors said they gave only 20 to 30 seconds to a perusal of the cover letter.

In that short window of opportunity, a job applicant should try to accomplish four things:

◆ Name the job you want. Major companies may be advertising for dozens of different jobs on a given day. The cover letter must specify a particular job so that the application can be routed correctly within the company.

◆ Tell briefly where you heard about the job. If you're responding to an advertisement, tell where it appeared. If a company employee or mutual acquaintance told you about the opening, mention his or her name (with permission).

◆ Highlight one or two aspects of your resume that would be particularly interesting or impressive to the company. Don't try to repeat your resume. Your goal in the cover letter is to emphasize aspects of the resume so that they will stand out when the resume is read.

◆ Ask for an interview. You can increase your chances of obtaining an interview by sounding enthusiastic and indicating your flexibility as to interview time and place.

In the following cover letter, the job applicant has seen an ad in the *Washington Post*. She mentions the name of the newspaper, the date, and the advertisement number (not all ads have numbers) to aid the company in routing her application correctly.

June 19, 20__

Herbert R. Signum
Director of Personnel
General Manufacturing, Inc.
983 Seventh St.
Washington, DC 20883

Dear Mr. Signum:

I'm eager to be considered for the Public Relations staff position advertised in the *Washington Post*, June 18, advertisement #292.

As my attached resume suggests, I have worked in positions of progressive responsibility in the public relations area since receiving my B.A. in Marketing from Georgetown University. You may be particularly interested in my leadership role in two high-profile PR projects at Apple Computer: the "Take a Byte" campaign and the "Easy as Pie" program for school sales.

I'll be happy to meet with you at your convenience to learn more about your goals for public relations at General Manufacturing and to introduce myself more thoroughly. Feel free to call me at my office (202-555-2893) or at home (391-555-4893). Thank you for considering my strong desire to interview for this position.

Sincerely,

Nancy R. Jenson

Nancy R. Jenson
Public Relations Specialist

Objections

What do you say (or keep from saying) when you disagree with the boss? For lack of an answer to that question, many managers bite their tongues and simply stew. They would be far better off if they were to explain their objections in a clear, respectful memo or letter.

In the following memo, a manager writes the most difficult objection of all—a challenge to the boss on a matter of ethics. The writer's goal is to stimulate the boss's thinking without awakening his ire. But above all, the writer wants to take a stand for the sake of her own conscience and, ultimately, for the welfare of the company.

July 16, 20__

  To: Sean Thomas
       Director of Personnel

From: Alice Trent
       Financial Analyst

Subject: Reconsideration of Recruitment Language

Sean, I'm concerned about a matter that involves both of our areas of responsibility. I'd like to explain my perspective on the subject and then to get your response.

As you know, we're under pressure as a company to show at least 50 employees with M.S. degrees on staff by August 1. Without them, we cannot qualify for federal contract #17A6, which requires this level of staff expertise when the federal contract is awarded.

Motivated by this pressure, your group has undertaken an aggressive recruitment campaign in the Silicon Valley region of California. Applications have begun to arrive from many California managers holding M.S. degrees.

At the same time, we're both aware from the CEO's internal document #8091 that layoffs of approximately 10 percent of the workforce will begin on September 15 of this year.

The dilemma as I see it, Sean, is that we are knowingly recruiting men and women who will sell their homes and move their families across country to take positions with our company—positions that will evaporate as soon as we have qualified for minimum M.S. staffing levels for the federal contract.

No matter what the pressures upon us, I believe our present course is both manipulative and ethically indefensible. The most obvious losers in this situation will be the many employees who move across country for what turns out to be no more than 45 days of work. But the company stands to lose as well, I think, when this situation appears in the press (as it will) and is reviewed by federal contract regulators.

So for all these reasons—human, ethical, and practical—I urge you to reconsider the current recruitment strategy. I don't have a solution to this dilemma, Sean, but I see a train wreck ahead on the company's present track. I welcome your opinion on the matter.

COMMUNICATION DURING CRISIS

Most of the communication lessons in this book assume a normal workday, with time to plan, think, draft, and revise. But it will come as no surprise to you that many workdays are far from normal. Market shifts, product failures, management changes, layoffs, and other unexpected events can make communication tasks absolutely urgent at the same time that you have little time to prepare them.

When, in a moment of crisis, you are required to provide some kind of written or oral communication, ask yourself four questions—and then abide by your answers.

1. *What is my purpose?* No single message can accomplish all possible purposes. You must select the one or two main purposes that your message drives toward. For example, your primary purpose may be to defend your company against unwarranted

charges. Or your purpose may be to inform your workforce and others about rumored changes in the company. Whatever your overarching purpose, keep it steadily in mind as you develop your message. Make sure that your message comes through by stating it clearly at both the beginning and the end of your communication (places at which the audience can be expected to be most attentive).

2. *Who is my audience?* You can't choose examples, vocabulary, or even the medium of your communication (letter, speech, e-mail, and so on) without knowing your audience well. Think in advance about what your audience wants to get from your communication. What do they need to hear? What will they do with the information you provide? Is your audience made up of subgroups, each with its own needs? How can you successfully address these subgroups while also communicating with the entire audience? Such audience analysis and planning rescues you from a potentially disastrous focus on "what I want to say" and moves you wisely in the direction of "what I want them to hear [or read]."

3. *What are my constraints?* In a crisis situation, time itself can be a constraint. You may have only a few minutes to think about your message before a microphone is stuck in your face and TV cameras begin to broadcast your words to hundreds of thousands of people. In the case of a written document, you may face time pressure in getting out a press release or other statement regarding a company development, product failure, leadership change, or other issue.

You probably also face legal constraints when developing messages in a crisis situation. An apology on behalf of the company, for example, may need to be drafted with great care (and reviewed by legal staff) so as not to admit inadvertently liability or culpability on the company's part. If you work for a company with publicly traded stock, the content and timing of your message must be wisely chosen so as not to affect the stock price in illegal ways.

Finally, you no doubt face resource constraints in crisis messages. Although you may want to get your company explanation out to as wide an audience as possible, you may often find that television, radio, and newspaper bureaus aren't eager to give you airtime or page space for free. Companies often have to buy full-page newspaper ads or pay for expensive media commercial time to counteract negative stories and get their explanations and justifications before the public.

4. *What are my chain-of-command constraints?* Imagine for a moment that you are a midlevel manager who knows virtually everything about why a particular company product failed in use and was lambasted by a consumer magazine. Your knowledge alone does not automatically make you the right person to communicate with the public on behalf of the company. In fact, employees are regularly told at such times to refer all inquiries to the company's public information officer or the CEO's office. At times of crisis, the company simultaneously wants to give what information it can to the public (to avoid the appearance of stonewalling) while protecting itself against free-wheeling investigations and unfounded charges.

When you have considered these guiding questions, rely on your own integrity and sincerity to speak or write your message clearly, succinctly, and even-handedly. Displays of anger, sarcasm, or inappropriate humor usually backfire at times when people seek serious answers to urgent questions.

SUMMARY KEYS TO DIFFICULT COMMUNICATIONS

Doing two or more dances at once leads inevitably to stumbling. In the same way, trying to be all things to all people in problematic business communications leads to writer's block or awkward expression.

Difficult communication becomes easier when the writer

◆ takes a stand;

◆ communicates that position in a tactful but straightforward way;

◆ conveys respect for the reader's motives and abilities.

Finally, trust a friend to read your draft of a difficult communication before you send it.

Appendices

◆

APPENDIX A:
A Quick Guide to Grammar and Punctuation

This concise guide limits its scope to practical problems faced by business writers. For a more complete grammar of the English language, refer to one of the comprehensive handbooks listed in Appendix C.

SENTENCES MUST BE COMPLETE

English sentences are composed of a subject (a noun or pronoun) and a predicate (containing a verb).

(noun)	(verb)
Western Electric	*explored fiber optics*
(subject)	(predicate)

Nouns name people (Clark Kent), places (Cincinnati), things (boxes), ideas (freedom), and activities (thinking).

Verbs describe action (pushes, sends, reaches) and states of beings (is, are, was, were).

Commands ("Go for coffee.") are complete sentences, though they seem to be missing a subject. The subject *you* is implied:

| *(You)* | *Go for coffee* |
| (implied subject) | (predicate) |

When a group of words lacks either a subject or a predicate, the result is a sentence fragment, not a sentence.

Fragment: And walked aimlessly for hours. (no subject)

Fragment: The man who left his briefcase in the car. (no predicate)

While advertising and magazine writers use sentence fragments freely, traditional business prose does not usually allow sentence fragments.

SENTENCES MUST BE DISTINCT

When two sentences run together as one, the result is a **run-on sentence**.

Error: Sandra gave creative energy to the company she sparked the imaginations of others by using her own.

When a writer unsuccessfully tries to repair a run-on sentence by using only a comma, the result is a **comma splice**.

Error: Sandra gave creative energy to the company, she sparked the imaginations of others by using her own.

Run-on sentences and comma splices can easily be repaired in any one of six ways.

1. Separate the two sentences with a period.

   Error: The mills needed raw materials the workers needed jobs.
   Correct: The mills needed raw materials. The workers needed jobs.

2. Join the two sentences with a semicolon.

   Example: The mills needed raw materials; the workers needed jobs.

3. Join the two sentences with a comma and a conjunction.

   Example: The mills needed raw materials, and the workers needed jobs.

4. Join the two sentences with a semicolon and a conjunctive adverb followed by a comma.

Example: The mills needed raw materials; however, the workers needed jobs.

Common conjunctive adverbs

accordingly	besides	hence	likewise	otherwise
also	consequently	however	moreover	still
anyhow	finally	indeed	nevertheless	then
anyway	furthermore	instead	next	therefore

5. Join the two sentences with a subordinate conjunction.

Example: The workers needed jobs because the mills needed raw materials.

Common subordinating conjunctions
Time: before, after, since, until, till, when, whenever, while, as
Place: where, wherever
Manner: as if, like
Reason: because, as, so that
Contrast: though, although, even though
Condition: if, unless, whether

6. Join the two sentences with a relative pronoun.

Error: Bernard Clay is an engineer, he banished the slide rule from our offices.
Correct: Bernard Clay is the engineer who banished the slide rule from our offices.

Common relative pronouns

who	which	this
whom	whose	that

SENTENCES MUST BE ORDERLY

Sentences must have their parts in the right places to work properly.

Error: Sarah placed both hands on the lectern, rising to speak.
(The lectern is not rising to speak!)

Correct: Rising to speak, Sarah placed both hands on the lectern.
Sarah, rising to speak, placed both hands on the lectern.

Phrases such as "rising to speak" add extra meaning to (or modify) the subject of the sentence, "Sarah." Always keep such modifiers close to the words they modify, to prevent distorted and silly meanings.

Error: He left his car behind, smoking a cigar.
Correct: Smoking a cigar, he left his car behind.

A modifier is said to "dangle" when added incorrectly at the beginning or end of a sentence:

Error: You can buy the watch at a discount price, which has a platinum bracelet.

Error: Together with the platinum bracelet, you can buy the watch at a discount price.

Correct: You can buy the watch with the platinum bracelet at a discount price.

SUBJECT AND VERB MUST AGREE

By acquired habit as speakers of English, we usually choose verbs that agree with the subjects in our sentences.

Factories sometimes cost (*not* costs) too much in the suburbs.
 (plural)   (plural)

Each of the workers leaves (*not* leave) at 5 p.m.
 (singular)   (singular)

Sometimes, however, we trip up by attaching a singular subject to a plural verb or vice versa.

Other easily mistaken singular subjects are

◆ Either/or

   Example: Either Jill or Mary answers our needs.

◆ Everyone

   Example: Everyone knows the head supervisor.

◆ Subjects separated by *or*

   Example: The computer or the teletype causes [not cause] static on the telephone.

Some plural nouns have singular meanings.

   Example: Economics is difficult but enlightening.
   (singular)

Other plural nouns include *aesthetics, checkers, mathematics, mumps, physics, politics,* and *statistics* (when referred to as a field of study).

Collective nouns can take singular or plural verbs, depending on whether they refer to a group as a unit or as a collection of individuals.

The team was organized by Henderly. (a group)
The team play their hearts out every game. (individuals)

PRONOUN CHOICE
Pronouns in a sentence must agree with the noun to which they refer.

Every one of the packages lost its wrapper.
(*not* their)

1. Use a plural pronoun to refer to two nouns joined by *and*.

   Wilson and Anderson gave their resignation speeches together.

   Use a singular pronoun to refer to subjects preceded by *each* or *every*.

   Each manager and each supervisor gave his or her approval to the project.

2. Use a singular pronoun to refer to nouns separated by *either/or* or *neither/nor*.

   Either the door or the hallway needs its annual coat of paint.

   When a singular and a plural noun are separated by *or*, the pronoun reference (and verb form) agrees with the noun closest to the verb.

   Common stock or apartments seem to be likely investment vehicles if their value remains steady this year.
   Apartments or common stock seems to be a likely investment vehicle if its value remains steady this year.

3. Use a singular or a plural pronoun to agree with collective nouns such as *committee, crew, group, majority, number,* and *team*, depending on whether it refers to a group as one unit or as a collection of independent individuals.

   The crew wins another of its many races.
   The crew are ready to receive their ribbons.

4. Use a singular pronoun to refer to *everyone*.

   Everyone has a right to express his or her own opinion.

5. Use a singular pronoun to refer to *some* or *most*, depending on whether *some* or *most* refers to singular or plural nouns.

Some of the sport has lost its excitement.
Some of the sports have lost their excitement.

6. Use *I, we, you, he, she, it,* and *they* as subjects.

He, she, and I went to the personnel office.

Note that these same forms are used after linking verbs:

The best worker is she. (She is the best worker.)

7. Use *me, us, you, him, her, it,* and *them* as direct objects, indirect objects, and objects of prepositions.

The job affected him and her in positive ways.
Send Tom and me the bill.
Send the bill to Tom and me.

8. Use *who* as a subject.

Who tells the boss what to do?
I want to meet the person who tells the boss what to do.

9. Use *whom* as an object.

Give the package to whom you wish.

10. The indefinite pronouns *few, several,* and *all* take plural verbs and pronoun references.

Few of the employees dislike their bosses.
Several of their friends board their pets.
All the boxes still sit in their appropriate places.

Indefinite pronouns such as *none* and *someone* take singular verbs and pronoun references.

None of the men knows his grandfather's place of birth.
Someone continues to leave his or her coat on my chair.

COMMA

Use a comma

1. To set off an introductory phrase or subordinate clause from the independent statement

When she saw the computer display, she noticed how little space it took on the top of the desk.

2. Before a coordinating conjunction (*and, or, but, for, yet,* or *nor*) linking two independent clauses; if the independent clauses are very short, the comma may be omitted

Landscaping for company headquarters may prove to be expensive, but first impressions of the company are often important for new clients.

3. After a conjunctive adverb following a semicolon

The staff members agree to work extra hours for three weeks; however, they requested overtime pay.

4. To set off nonrestrictive (or nonessential) phrases or clauses

One of our managers, who knew PASCAL, offered to help debug the program.

5. To set off phrases or words in apposition

John Wilson, candidate for Congress, spoke at the luncheon.

6. To set off a name directly addressed

We will expect your letter, Ms. Jones, no later than September 5.

7. To set off an interjection

Well, I see your point.

8. To separate adjectives in a series

For our service truck, we sought an inexpensive, dependable vehicle.

9. To set off quoted material from the rest of a sentence

"We can meet our goals," proclaimed the new president.

10. To precede the conjunction when a list of three or more items is given

The clips, brads, and fasteners were in the drawer.

SEMICOLONS

1. Use semicolons to separate closely related main clauses.

Creative business managers know how to delegate authority; they give their employees a sense of importance by involving them in significant ways.

2. Use semicolons to separate items in complex lists.

The assembly line faced a variety of problems: workers who, left by themselves, wasted time; machinery that dated from the Eisenhower years; and rushed schedules that brought perpetual panic.

COLONS

1. Use colons to signal the introduction of an example, an explanation, a quotation, or a list. Colons should always follow complete sentences.

   Error: The ingredients of the concrete: Portland cement, lime, sand, pea gravel, and water.

   Correct: The ingredients of the concrete were the following: Portland cement, lime, sand, pea gravel, and water.

2. Use colons in time designations and after greetings in formal letters.

   The workday begins promptly at 8:00 A.M.
   Dear Ms. McCoy:

APOSTROPHES

1. Use apostrophes to mark missing letters in contractions.

   isn't   they've   she's

2. Use apostrophes to form some plurals.

   Ph.D.'s   C.O.D.'s

3. Use apostrophes to indicate possession.

Singular:	business's	boss's	manager's	woman's
Plural:	businesses'	bosses'	managers'	women's

   a. It's = it is
      It's important to me.
      Its = belongs to it
      The table is missing its leg.

b. Personal pronouns (hers, theirs, ours) do not take apostrophes.

The job is hers if she wants it.

c. The impersonal pronoun *one* uses an apostrophe.
One's work can also be one's recreation.

QUOTATION MARKS

1. Use quotation marks to separate others' words from your own.

He called out, "Please step forward if you wish to bid."

2. Use quotation marks to set off titles of short poems, short stories, songs, chapters, essays, or articles.

"How to Write a Résumé"   "The Lake Isle of Innisfree"

3. Use quotation marks to indicate irony.

His "university degree" was in fact a diploma purchased for $300.

Be careful not to overuse quotation marks in this way.

ITALICS

1. Use italics (or underlining) to mark the titles of books, plays, movies, newspapers, and magazines.

The Wall Street Journal reviewed the financial aspects of *Star Wars*.

2. Use italics to identify foreign words and phrases.

The visitor used the German word for work, *arbeiten*.

3. Use italics to give special emphasis.

We asked the supervisor not only *how* to do the job, but *why* it should be done at all.

4. Use italics to set off words that you wish to call attention to as words.

Tell the technical writers they use *is* too often.

PARENTHESES

1. Use parentheses to enclose explanation or details.

The 507 press (a fabrication press for plywood) saved the company $82,000 in one year.

2. Use parentheses to enclose publisher information in a footnote.

John Renley, *Common Stock Investment Strategies* (New York: Williams Press, 2003).

DASHES

1. Use dashes to separate a series from the rest of the sentence.

The essential materials of the automobile—steel, rubber, plastic, and glass—can be stockpiled in almost unlimited quantities.

2. Use dashes to mark off an afterthought.

Her resignation came only after repeated attempts to get the raise she wanted—and deserved, for that matter.

3. Use dashes to separate a parenthetical comment or to show an abrupt break in the sentence.

Ledger books—the kind used for professional bookkeeping—were being sold at half price.

HYPHENS

1. Use hyphens to mark divisions within hyphenated words.

editor-in-chief   twenty-one (but one hundred and five)

2. Use hyphens to divide words into syllables when division is necessary at a line-end.

cor-   corpo-   corpora-
poration   ration   tion

CAPITALIZATION

1. Use a capital letter to begin sentences, direct quotations, and most lines of poetry.

Let your employees feel that they matter.
He asked, "Why did you call?"

2. Capitalize the names and initials of persons, places, and geographical areas.

Henry Higgins   Hinton, Iowa   the South

3. Capitalize the names of organizations and their members.

Rotary Club   Rotarians

4. Capitalize the names of ships, planes, and spacecraft.

Voyager II   the *Queen Elizabeth*

5. Capitalize the names of ethnic groups, races, nationalities, religions, languages, and historical periods.

> Jewish   Romanian   Native American
> English   Renaissance

6. Capitalize the names of days, months, holidays, and historical periods and events.

> Friday   October   the Roaring Twenties   Memorial Day

7. Capitalize the first word and all other major words in titles of books, plays, poems, musical compositions, films, and works of art.

> "Some Enchanted Evening"
> *The Sound and the Fury*   *Star Wars*

◆

APPENDIX B:
Converting Written Documents to Oral Presentations

Excellent reports and proposals in written form often lead to an invitation from senior management to present this material orally, perhaps to a meeting or convention. Learning to convert fine writing into fine speaking involves much more than simply reading your document aloud. This guide will lead you step-by-step through the process that leads to speaking success.

STEP ONE:
Analyze your audience—again
The audience for whom you wrote your document may differ significantly from the audience who will hear your oral presentation. Take a few moments, therefore, to think through the experience of your audience, their intellectual or educational level, their attention spans, and their attitudes and beliefs. Make adjustments in your speech based on what you discover about your audience.

STEP TWO:
Understand the ten commandments of effective presenting

◆ Speak up.

◆ Get to the point early.

◆ Gesture naturally.

◆ Vary your volume, pitch, and tone.

◆ Organize your speech.

◆ Use direct eye contact.

◆ Pause effectively.

◆ Speak at a comfortable pace.

◆ Use appropriate visual aids.

◆ Listen to what your audience is telling you verbally and nonverbally.

STEP THREE:
Channel speaker's nerves into energetic presenting

Few of us fear what is actually happening prior to or during a presentation. After all, we're not literally threatened by physical danger at such moments. Instead, we fear what might happen. This fear is called anticipatory anxiety. We plague ourselves by worrying what others might think, what nervous symptoms we'll experience, whether others will notice those symptoms, whether we'll remember what to say, whether we'll look too fat or too thin or too tall or too short. These worries, and many more, make public speaking one of the most feared of life's events—more feared, in some recent surveys, than death itself.

The solution to speaker's nerves is not, surprisingly, to "make nerves go away." Even the most experienced presenters reveal that they still feel the surge of excitement, extra adrenalin, and heightened bodily sensations prior to a speech. But these feelings, so feared by beginning presenters, have been reinterpreted by experienced speakers as a help, not a hindrance, to effective speaking. Channeled correctly, nervous energy can give life and high interest to a speaker's manner and delivery.

Learning to transform nervous symptoms from hindrance to help involves four steps:

1. *Prepare* You can take away at least half of speaking worries simply by knowing what you want to say, why you want to say it, and to whom you're speaking.

2. *Practice* Each speaking experience can desensitize you for future speaking. Knowing that you survived one speaking experience can give you confidence that you'll get through others as well—and perhaps even begin to enjoy them.

3. *Keep your mind on your task* Worrying about the beating of your heart or the rapidity of your breathing or your sweaty palms will only increase whatever symptoms bother you in these areas. Learn to focus intensely on what you're communicating to your audience.

4. *Remember that your audience appreciates your humanness more than your perfection* Let yourself be yourself, even to the point of laughing a bit at your own nerves or admitting your nervousness to your audience. Facing up to your nerves instead of trying to hide them is one of the best ways to channel panic into an energetic delivery.

STEP FOUR:

Five effective openings for capturing your listener's attention
Good speeches usually do not begin with the same language used in the documents from which they grew. How you choose to begin an oral presentation determines in large part your listeners' attitudes toward you and your subject. No single opening is right for all speaking occasions. As with all communication experiences, you must analyze your audience, purpose, and occasion to find just the

right beginning for your speech. Openings should be relatively brief, pointed toward your theme, and interesting. Consider these five popular openers:

1. *Ask a question* You can wake up your audience and heighten their interest in your topic by posing an interesting question. For example, "How many of you would be willing to sacrifice five percent of your salary for the right to work from home two days out of the week?"

2. *Begin with a quotation* As a speaker, you can often associate yourself with prestigious company by a well-chosen quotation: "Lyndon Johnson, a true friend to American business, defined 'business ethics' in this way: 'Do business today in the way you want your children to do business tomorrow.'"

3. *Reveal an interesting visual aid* We are an increasingly visual culture, often preferring film and TV images to the spoken and written word. A well-chosen video clip, slide, or physical object can rivet the attention of your audience. Prior to a speech for charity, for example, a speaker might begin by asking the audience to watch silently as images of needy children appear on the screen.

4. *Tell an affecting personal story* We all love stories, particularly those that end up with a powerful point or a surprise. In giving a speech on sagging company profits, for example, one manager told a charming story about his first business failure—a lemonade stand for which the materials and ingredients cost much more than his eventual sales.

5. *Use appropriate humor* Audiences are eager to "loosen up" at the beginning of a presentation. Oblige them by recounting a humorous experience or telling a joke. The humor must not seem canned, however, and should not violate the norms of good taste.

Lee Iaccocca began one of his many public speeches by telling the hilarious story of how several company managers became trapped inside a new mini-van as it rolled out before TV cameras for the first time.

STEP FIVE:
Structuring your business presentation

A business presentation should grab attention from the start. Along with a personal introduction and greeting, a business presenter often uses a personal story, a riveting visual aid, an arresting fact, a joke, or a relevant anecdote to catch attention and build rapport.

From that point on, the nature of topics treated and the method of topic development will depend largely on the speaker's analysis of his or her audience. From that analysis emerges a pattern of organization that will make the speech "hang together" (that is, be clear at all major points) for the audience. Common patterns of organization include the following:

The Problem-Solution Presentation
  I.   Introduction
  II. Description/Analysis of the Problem
  III. Review of Attempted Solutions from the Past
  IV. Evaluation of What Is Needed Now
  V.   Recommendation for Action

The Information Presentation
  I.   Introduction
  II. What We Already Know, and Why
  III. What We Need to Know, and Why
  IV. Presentation of Needed Information
  V.   Conclusion, with Recommendation(s)

The Interpretive Presentation
  I. Introduction
  II. The Present Situation
  III. How It Came About
  IV. What We Can Do About It
  V. Conclusion, with Recommendation(s)

Conclude the business presentation with a summary statement that answers the question, "So what?" (that is, so what if all you have said in the presentation is true? What does it add up to?). In many cases, the answer to the "so what?" question is a call to action, in which the presenter urges the audience to take a defined course of action.

STEP SIX:
Use anecdotes effectively
Anecdotes are short accounts of interesting or humorous incidents. They are ideal for opening a business speech, if they are appropriate to the occasion, audience, speaker, and topic. Anecdotes give the audience a sense of fun rather than work, help to establish rapport between the speaker and audience, and do a great deal to humanize the speaker's message. Chosen well, anecdotes can prove a powerful ally in communicating the speaker's theme. Because anecdotes are memorable for the audience, the same themes or characters in the anecdote may reappear later in the speech as a summary of an idea or the reinforcement of a point.

STEP SEVEN:
Plan for successful luncheon or after dinner speeches
These speaking occasions can prove crucial for upward career mobility. Often they provide a venue for the speaker to reach not

only his or her superiors within the company but also influential community and industry leaders.

The after dinner speech is usually intended to give pleasure and instruction, in that order. Audiences typically expect the speaker to draw upon personality, genial wit, and a gift for storytelling in making his or her after dinner speech a memorable, but not difficult, listening experience. These guidelines may assist you:

1. Determine in advance what topics will interest and please your audience.

2. Plan humorous moments in your speech that apply directly to the main topic or theme.

3. Speak directly and simply, without unnecessary complication and with a minimum of difficult concepts or hard vocabulary.

4. Make sparing use of statistics, charts, or graphs that may tax a relaxed, somewhat weary audience beyond its limits of attention and concentration.

5. Keep to the time allotted for your speech.

6. Provide initial, internal, and final summaries so your audience clearly grasps your point.

♦

APPENDIX C:
References for Further Reading

American Psychological Association. *Publication Manual of the American Psychological Association,* 5th Ed. Washington, DC: American Psychological Association, 2001.

Bird, Drayton. *How to Write Sales Letters That Sell,* 2nd Ed. London: Kogan Page Ltd, 2003.

Bresler, Kenneth. *The Workplace Writing Workbook.* Buffalo, NY: Hein, 2003.

Brown, Ralph. *Making Business Writing Happen.* Australia: Allen & Unwin, 2003.

Economists Press Staff. *The Economist Style Guide,* 8th Ed. Gainesville, FL: Economists Books, 2003.

Freed, Richard. *Writing Winning Business Proposals,* 2nd Ed. New York: McGraw-Hill, 2003.

Gibaldi, J. *The MLA Style Manual and Guide to Scholarly Publishing,* 2nd Ed. New York: Modern Language Association, 1998.

Hershkowitz-Coore, Sue. *Power Sales Writing.* New York: McGraw-Hill, 2003.

Martin, Paul. *The Wall Street Journal Essential Guide to Business Style and Usage.* New York: Wall Street Journal, 2003.

Public Library Association. *The Guide to Basic Cover Letter Writing,* 2nd Ed. New York: McGraw-Hill, 2003.

Roy, Jennifer. *You Can Write a Business Letter.* Berkeley Heights, NJ: Enslow, 2003.

Ryan, Kevin. *Write Up the Corporate Ladder.* New York: AMACOM, 2003.

Sant, Tom. *Persuasive Business Proposals*, 2nd Ed. New York: AMACOM, 2003.

Starkey, Lauren B. *Goof-Proof Business Writing*. Florence, KY: Delmar, 2003.

Tremore, Judy. *The Everything Grant Writing Book*. Avon, MA: Adams Media Corp., 2003.

United States Government Printing Office Style Manual. Washington, DC: Government Printing Office, 2000.

University of Chicago Press Staff. *Chicago Manual of Style,* 15th Ed. Chicago: University of Chicago Press, 2003.

INDEX